About the Authors

Ginna Bell Bragg is the chef and nutritional expert for The Chopra Center for Well Being in La Jolla, California.

David Simon, MD, has studied Ayurveda with Deepak Chopra for more than ten years. At present he oversees the research wing of The Institute for Human Potential and Mind Body Medicine and provides direction for all clinical programmes offered at The Chopra Center for Well Being.

GINNA BELL BRAGG & DAVID SIMON

THE
AYURVEDIC
COOKBOOK

VEGETARIAN
RECIPES FOR BODY,
MIND AND SPIRIT

FOREWORD BY
DEEPAK CHOPRA

RIDER
LONDON · SYDNEY · AUCKLAND · JOHANNESBURG

First published in 1997

1 3 5 7 9 10 8 6 4 2

First published in 1997 by Harmony Books, a division of Crown Publishers, Inc., 201 East 50th Street, New York, New York 10022.

Published in Great Britain in 1997 by Rider,
an imprint of Ebury Press, Random House,
20 Vauxhall Bridge Road, London SW1V 2SA

Random House Australia (Pty) Limited
20 Alfred Street, Milsons Point, Sydney,
New South Wales 2061, Australia

Random House New Zealand Limited
18 Poland Road, Glenfield,
Auckland 10, New Zealand

Random House South Africa (Pty) Limited
Endulini, 5A Jubilee Road, Parktown 2193, South Africa

Random House UK Limited Reg. No. 954009

Papers used by Rider Books are natural, recyclable products made from wood grown in sustainable forests.

Typeset by SX Composing DTP, Rayleigh, Essex
Printed by Mackays of Chatham, Kent

A CIP catalogue record for this book is available from the British Library

ISBN 0-7126-7214-1

*To Sister Mary Helen, O.P., who opened
my mind; to Sister Mary Augustine,
O.P., who planted my feet on a creative
path; and to Sister Mary Burns,
O.P., who gave me wings.*

God Bless You.

G.B.B.

ACKNOWLEDGEMENTS

My first thanks must go posthumously to my parents, Virginia and Richard Bragg, both artists, whose union provided the mix of chromosomes that created me. Thank you for your undying love, even now;

to my son, Michael, whose management, hugs and cups of tea have sustained me;

to my dear friends Ken Gregg, Fred Coleman, Sampson Bowers, Rachel Coleman and Rick Dinihanian, all of whom provided money, loyalty and encouragement to bring me to this moment;

to my brothers, Mark and Jess Bragg, and my lovely sisters-in-law, Pegge and Patty, whose devotion and kind words know no bounds;

to my girlfriends Nan Heflin, Mary Kay Fry and Toni Ahlgren, whose wonder at and joy of life gave me constant courage to go on; and John Lyle, dear companion;

to Caroline Graham Muir, who introduced me to Bragg's Liquid Aminos, and the rest is history;

to John Gladstein and his mountaintop Rainbow Ranch, my starting point;

to Muriel Nellis, agent extraordinaire, and to Shaye Areheart, our editor, Dina Siciliano, her assistant, and all the good people at Harmony Books, for their knowledge and support;

to Barbara St. George, Mary Horner and Johnathan Copenhaver, my original Center staff, for their faithful observance of kitchen consciousness; and Chris Saxon Barley, whose assistance in service, photographs and transcriptions was invaluable;

to my most conscious spiritual advisers, Revs. Joan Gattuso and Jane Meyers, whose over-the-phone meditations and guidance brought peace into my heart at the most intense moments, and whose example as spiritual beings encourages me to "walk my talk";

to David, who saw me, knew me and gave light to this book;

to Peter, who just plain loves me;

to Deepak, for inspiration;

and to Great Spirit, for the gift of this life.

Namasté.

Ginna Bell Bragg

My love and appreciation flow to the many celestial souls who have provided me with love and nourishment along my journey:

to my mother and father, Lee Shirley and Myron, for their unconditional nurturing;

to my brother, Howard, for his unconditional sharing;

to my beloved son, Max, for his unconditional mirroring;

to Pamela, for her unconditional love;

to my many dear friends and colleagues at The Chopra Center for Well Being and Infinite Possibilities International for their commitment to the embodiment of Spirit;

to the Divine Mother incarnation, Ginna, for her culinary alchemy;

and to my dear friend, brother and teacher, Deepak, for his unwavering pursuit of the miraculous.

Love and light,

David Simon

CONTENTS

FOREWORD

'Food is Brahman,' proclaim the ancient Vedic texts. Brahman is consciousness, and the physical body that we inhabit for the time being is condensed consciousness. The mind is a field of ideas. The body is a field of molecules. One is consciousness in thought form, the other is consciousness in material form, but the two are aspects of the same field of pure intelligence in different disguises.

Consciousness curving back within itself creates ego, intellect, mind, the physical body and the experience of the material world. This, declare the great sages, is the process through which the seer becomes the scenery, the observer becomes the observed and the creator becomes the creation. Creator and creation are one. Food is Brahman.

You may look at an item of food and see only its colour and form, experience only its texture or taste. But food is an expression of the same universal mind that creates your body and has the same levels of manifestation that comprise your physical form. Ayurvedic texts declare that you have a physical body made up of matter and energy, a subtle body made up of mind, intellect and ego, and a causal body made up of soul and spirit. When you look at a banana or a glass of orange juice, you may not fully grasp that there is *prana,* or universal energy, there, or that the same spirit that animates everything that lives, moves or breathes exists in food, but it's there all the same.

From the state of being we begin to experience the material universe as our extended body. Then nature is no longer something to be conquered, subjugated and exploited. When we are ready to have an intimate relationship with the womb of creation that is Mother Earth, we will be healed. More than anything else, modern nutrition needs to understand that food is not mere calories, proteins, fats, minerals and vitamins. Food is intelligence. We are intelligence and we are in constant and dynamic exchange with universal intelligence through physiological processes, of which eating is the most important. Eating, digestion and metabolism are the transformation of one mode of intelligence into another. The life energy in a kernel of corn today may become a light receptor in your eye tomorrow, which decodes the intelligence of the universe into colour and form. When we understand the miracle of life and begin to comprehend that life feeds upon itself to transform itself into different manifestations, we will begin to have some insight into the magic and miracle of living. Life is a miracle. Eating is a miracle. We begin as a speck of information on a DNA molecule, food is added, and that same food is transformed into our brain, intellect and ego, which begins to ask itself: 'Who am I? Where do I come from? What is the meaning of my existence?'

All the great wisdom traditions of the world have looked upon the miracle of nutrition as something sacred. If we could understand this one idea – that the Absolute (spirit) transforms itself into the Relative (physical world) through its own self-sacrifice – eating would be elevated to the stature of a sacrament. When we develop reverence for food and the miracle of transformation inherent in it, just the simple act of eating creates a ritual of celebration. This is what we really need in our awareness – to make eating a celebration. Every disease that humans are prey to, from cardiovascular problems to cancer to degenerative disorders, has been linked in some way or another to diet. Despite this understanding, our approach to diet to date has been clinical, sterile and void of the mystery of life that is present in every act of eating. Modern nutritional science looks at food as a dead substance that can be quantified in calories and described by its biochemical constituents. A vast number of our population are sustained by so-called nutrients that are imprisoned for extended periods of time in tins or frozen packages. There is no life energy in eating this food, but science smugly declares that it contains everything our bodies need. As long as our approach to life is technical, we will remain mere technicians. Our physicians are no longer healers but great technicians who know almost everything about the human body but practically nothing about the human soul. We require a transformation that can only be called holy. We need to transform the way we look at life itself and in that transformation we will remember that food, too, has a soul.

This book is about food for the soul. It is about the celebration of nourishment at all levels: physical, mental and spiritual. It is about wholeness and therefore about healing and that which is holy.

Ingest the knowledge in this book and digest it as you would a sumptuous meal and you will participate consciously in the cosmic dance of transformation. Every moment is full of energy, vitality, awareness and joy.

DEEPAK CHOPRA, M.D.

INTRODUCTION

Open Heart, Open Mind

GINNA: I love food and I love to cook. I love shopping for special ingredients, meeting local farmers and bakers, growing succulent vegetables and creating beautiful, health-supporting meals. When I first began my exploration of Ayurvedic cooking, I was deeply moved by the reverence this ancient healing system has for the value of nutritious food and the person who lovingly prepares it. The principle that nourishment comes from the love of the cook as well as the food on your plate completely resonated with my beliefs and experience.

DAVID: I love food and I love to eat. When I first tasted Ginna's fabulous cooking, I was delighted because I could actually taste the flavour of love in her food. I was so inspired that I recruited her to prepare the meals for our programme at The Chopra Center for Well Being.

GINNA: I was merrily cooking for retreats and workshops in northern California, living in a 400-square-foot tepee, when David came along with his taste buds. I was practising Ayurvedic principles in my kitchen – arising early, meditating, beginning each day with beautiful chants, music and the aroma of my favourite incense. The guests arriving for breakfast frequently commented on the healing and nourishing energy they received, even *before* they put food in their mouths.

DAVID: This makes sense because according to Ayurveda, the universe is a magnificent and magical web of energy and information. Each of our lives is a unique and dynamic design within the cosmic weaving. Our thoughts and feelings extend across time and space, so Ginna's consciousness and caring are tangible in and around her food.

GINNA: My true dharma, or purpose in life, is providing sustenance and nourishment for people along their path of spiritual growth. Nutritionally supporting and educating people at The Chopra Center for Well Being provide the opportunity to serve others while expressing my unique talents.

DAVID: When people make a commitment to transform and improve their lives, it is often reflected in their food choices. Whether you are recovering from an illness, changing jobs or relationships, or simply want to 'live healthier', food provides a tangible way to demonstrate your change. This book is dedicated to supporting and celebrating your progress on the path of increasing happiness and wholeness.

GINNA: My intention in collaborating on this book is not only to share recipes and ingredients, but to explore with you the spiritual and mindful aspects of cooking. To paraphrase Picasso, when I enter the kitchen, I leave my concerns outside the door, like a Muslim who removes his shoes before entering the mosque. In other words, I surrender to the task, giving my heart and soul to the preparation of a delicious meal. In this state, the cook, the preparation and the meal itself are seen as different expressions of the same creative force, motivated by love and the impulse to nourish.

DAVID: One of the important goals of this book is to demonstrate that it is easy to prepare delicious food that is enjoyable by Westerners and fully resonates with the principles of Ayurveda. We do not need to eat curries at every meal in order to enjoy a balanced, health-enhancing diet. The ancient mind-body principles of Ayurveda can be readily applied to dishes from every culture.

DAVID AND GINNA: We offer this book as an expression of our love. We hope it will inspire you to share your love through the preparation of food, whether it is for yourself or others. Preparing and sharing delicious and nutritious food is a celebration of both our uniqueness and our unity.

Chapter

1

HEART AND SOUL OF THE COOK

KITCHEN CONSCIOUSNESS — COOKING WITH LOVE

The artistic spirit in us all craves attractive surroundings, which inspire us to bring forth beautiful creations. Whatever we focus on in our lives – be it painting, writing, making music or cooking – there is a wonderful benefit to wrapping ourselves in warm, inviting, inspiring settings with comfortable chairs, healthy plants, beautiful music and the right books. Prop your feet up on the desk to read cookbooks; curl up in front of the fire to write down recipes.

The kitchen can be your studio for creating nourishing, beautiful meals for yourself and your family and friends. You don't need to be an artist or a professional cook to prepare fabulous food. All you need are fresh ingredients, a selection of herbs and spices, a sharp knife and love.

Love is the essential ingredient. It is the channel through which every good meal flows. Whether as cooks at home or as professional chefs, we are cooking to nourish the human race. When we contribute to the health, well-being and happiness of one individual, we are contributing to the health, well-being and happiness of the whole planet.

Every time someone eats a meal cooked with your love, they carry away with them a fuller heart and a more lively spirit. You are offering your best to those who can benefit from your love and attention.

Love of food begins with love of life. Ayurveda tells us that 'food is Brahman'. Brahman is pure potentiality. We are not only what we eat, we are the thoughts that go into what we eat. If what we eat has been cooked by an angry, hostile person, we ultimately take away with us their anger and hostility and give it back to the world. If we eat food prepared by someone filled with love and caring, these ingredients fill our body, mind and soul. Then we find it easiest to share the best of ourselves with those around us.

Ayurveda teaches us that the most satisfying and nourishing meals come from farmers who grow their crops with love, grocers who sell their produce with love and preparers who cook with love. Even if you cannot personally meet your food growers, choose your materials carefully, remembering that each ingredient is an essential part of the whole of your creation. If you begin with good whole ingredients, your salads will be fresher, your vegetable dishes more succulent and your breads more nourishing.

Whenever possible, we recommend the use of organic, locally grown produce but it may not always be possible to find it in your market. If this is the case, choose the best grains, flour, nuts, fruits and vegetables available and cook with love.

The herbs and spices in your kitchen can make or break a meal. Beautifully cut and stir-fried vegetables can be delightful if spiced just right, or unpalatable if spiced too heavily or with the wrong flavour. As we'll discuss in the next chapter, Ayurveda teaches that different people have different constitutions. By choosing the correct herb and spice combinations, or *churans,* we can enhance each person's mind-body balance. Following the recipes in this book, we have included a Balance of Tastes Chart (page 209) to help you choose the best herbs, spices and vegetables for your constitutional type.

According to Ayurveda, food should always be as fresh as possible. The life force, or *prana,* is most vital in meals that use fresh, recently prepared ingredients. Don't skimp when shopping for your meals. Always buy the best that is available. Day-old bread is only good for the bread crumbs you can make out of it. Use whole, beautiful, crispy vegetables and you will create the most tantalizing, savoury meals.

KITCHEN TANTRA

In our Ayurvedic cooking classes at The Chopra Center for Well Being, our highest priority is the consciousness we have while cooking – our state of mind and heart while in the kitchen. We like to call this *kitchen tantra.* Tantra is a Sanskrit word that means 'the fabric of life'. It is the understanding that every one of our thoughts, feelings and desires is connected to and interwoven with the whole of creation. In the West, tantra is most commonly associated with rituals of sexuality, but this is just one facet of this ancient spiritual science. A tantric approach integrates consciousness, mind and behaviour so that all our actions express our inherent spiritual nature. Kitchen tantra seeks to enliven the unity value of the cook, the cooking and the food. In this state, the life force of the preparer merges with the life force of the food to create delicious and life-affirming meals.

Kitchen tantra is a composition in consciousness with four-part harmony. These components are *Kriya,* or ritual; *Carya,* or demeanour; *Yoga,* or integration of mind, body and spirit; and *Anuttara,* or understanding.

Kriya (Ritual) Ritual captures our attention. Ritual in the kitchen reminds us that preparing food is a celebration of life. Perform some ritual when you are about to cook – light a candle, play music, arrange fresh flowers. Wash your hands and wipe the counter before you begin and again when you have completed the meal. Whatever you do to create your special space, to make the act of food preparation important, will contribute to the value of your meal.

Look at your kitchen as a studio designed for the creation of nourishment. Arrange your pots and pans, cooking utensils and food products in a pleasing, accessible way, as if they were your brushes, paint tubes and canvases. As Mother used to say, clean up as you go along and put things away in the same place each time you use them. Keep your knives sharpened, your towels clean and your aprons fresh.

Ritual in the kitchen can be as simple as a thought – a silent mental reminder that the kitchen you enter is a holy place. See it as your temple for the joyful creation of soups, the mindful preparation of bread dough, the genesis of a celestial dessert.

Carya (Demeanour) Your kitchen can be a place of delight and your demeanour while cooking is a key ingredient in your meals. Remember to be mindful, present and centred, focusing on the task. But don't be serious – be playful. The creative process is fun. According to Vedic knowledge, the entire universe was created for the fun of it. Cooking with a friend or beloved is a great way to express your love for each other and a fun way to play together. It also adds to the deliciousness of the meal. Be creative and open to new ideas. Trust your intuition. Be free.

Yoga (Integration) Food preparation is an opportunity to integrate body, mind and soul. Cooking can be a moving meditation – a dance in the studio of nourishment. Meditating before you cook is a good idea, but the act of cooking itself, especially when you are alone in the kitchen, can be a satisfying meditative experience. Be an open channel for inspiration, allowing yourself to experience the pure, creative force that lies within you. When you are in a creative, meditative state in the kitchen, the magic of healing flows through you and into your soup, your pasta and your simple fruit salads.

Anuttara (Understanding) When you bring the understanding of the masters into the kitchen, you bring balance, joy and the spirit of celebration. The knowledge from all spiritual traditions reminds us that underlying the diversity of name and form is unity. Let this understanding of our connectedness to each other and everything in creation flow through our mind and body into our fingers as we knead the bread dough, form it into loaves and place it in the oven. If we look at a carrot as an example of the beauty, simplicity and perfection of the universe, we see food from the perspective of a sage, illuminated mind.

The menu, ingredients and recipes are all important components of each meal. But your SELF is so vital to the task that you cannot for a moment lose track of it. To be conscious in the kitchen means to be fully aware of the picture of which you are a part. It is a painting in the works and you are the holder of the brush. You choose the colours, the types of paint and the canvas. When you stand before the empty canvas, become a clear channel through which the spirit of creation flows.

Anyone who can read and shop can follow a recipe. But the consciousness of the cook, the presence of holiness in the kitchen and the shared desire, by cook and guest, to be healthy world mates is something only love can provide. Be in love while cooking. Be love itself.

WHAT'S IN THE PANTRY?

The following is a general listing of ingredients most often used by Western cooks using Ayurvedic principles. We recommend that you always have them on hand, as so many of our recipes include them. Whenever possible, buy organic products. Refer to the Balance of Tastes Chart (page 209) for information regarding your specific constitutional needs.

Nonperishables

anise

arrowroot

asafoetida (hing)
  (an Ayurvedic spice
  resembling garlic)

basmati rice
  (naturally grown, very
  aromatic white rice)

bread crumbs

buckwheat

cardamom

churans (herb-spice
  blends)
  (Vata, Pitta, Kapha)

chilli paste or powder

cinnamon

cloves

coconut

coconut milk

coriander

corn

cumin

currants, raisins, sultanas

dates

dried minced onion

fennel seeds

flour
  (organic unbleached strong
  white flour and organic
  wholemeal flour for breads)
  (organic unbleached fine
  plain white and organic
  fine wholemeal flour for
  cakes and biscuits)

fruit, dried

chickpeas

ginger, ground

honey
  (pure unfiltered)

Italian Seasonings

kashi
  (cereal mix)

lentils
  (brown, red)

maple syrup

millet

miso

mung beans

mustard
  (dry, yellow)

nutmeg

nuts and seeds

oats

olive oil

oregano

peppercorns

pine nuts

quinoa

Rice Dream

rye

sea salt

sesame oil

soy sauce
   (use non-fermented, or
   light soy sauce)

split peas
   (yellow, green)

sugar
   (use natural (unrefined)
   sugar such as light brown
   soft sugar or light
   muscovado sugar)

tarragon

thyme

tomatoes, sun-dried

treacle

turmeric

vegetable bouillon
   powder

vegetable seasoning
   powder

yeast, dried fast acting

Perishables

apple juice
   (unfiltered)

butter

coriander, fresh

eggs

ghee
   (clarified butter)

lemons

limes

milk

orange juice

Paneer cheese

parsley, fresh

root ginger, fresh

tempeh

tofu

yoghurt
   (use low-fat, very low-fat or
   virtually fat-free plain
   yoghurt)

HOW, WHEN, WHAT TO BUY?

CHOOSING FRUIT AND VEGETABLES

Instead of relying on supermarkets and grocers, try to buy produce direct from farmers, or at farmers' markets, which are fun and *sattvic* (creative) places. Farmers love what they do, especially organic farmers who are conscious of their effect on the environment and our bodies.

Organic produce may not always look the prettiest, but it usually is the tastiest. Bruises or discolourations do not affect the flavour of the food. Look for the Soil Association Organic Standard or Organic Farmers & Growers label. Select small fruits and vegetables, which are the most flavourful. Large courgettes and pumpkins may look beautiful but tend to taste woody and bland. Choose delicate, young vegetables whenever possible.

GROWING YOUR OWN

Growing your own fruits and vegetables can be fun if you have the time and space. There are many wonderful books on the subject of organic gardening and useful tips on TV gardening programmes. Remember, too, to use your intuition. Plants have their own spirit which, when honoured, contributes greatly to the nourishment of the meal.

SEASONS

Whether store-bought or grown in your own garden, vegetables and fruits are best eaten in season. Using locally grown produce ensures that you are getting the freshest, most nutritious and least expensive ingredients. If the selection in local shops is poor – as it can be at some times of the year – purchase those fruits and vegetables that radiate the most life force. If they look and smell vital, they are most likely to taste fresh and delicious when eaten.

READING LABELS

When shopping in the supermarket, read the labels. If you can't pronounce a component, you probably don't want to eat it. Look for items that have whole ingredients, without preservatives or added salt.

CLEANING THE REFRIGERATOR

According to Ayurveda, food should be fresh, fresh, fresh. Throw out the leftovers in your refrigerator before they become science projects! No one really wants to eat them anyway. Eating food that is depleted of life force is wasting it.

NOURISHING FAMILY AND FRIENDS

Eating according to Ayurvedic principles means being more in tune with what is natural. Our society has lost this understanding because so many of us were raised on frozen meals in front of the television. People usually adapt to change if it is introduced one step at a time. Don't try to cram an Ayurvedic approach down your family's throat or you are sure to encounter resistance. The best way to influence those around you is by being an example. Begin with yourself. Prepare meals with all six tastes represented. Pay attention to the Body Intelligence Techniques (BITS) (page 18). Provide *churans* on the table for each dosha, or mind-body principle. As you begin to feel healthier and more vital, those around you will want to participate in a change that they perceive as beneficial. Relax and enjoy.

ENTERTAINING

Entertaining can be a rewarding time to express yourself artistically and Ayurvedically. Beautifully presented, balanced food feeds the soul as well as the body. Take the time to create an attractive table, using colours that enhance your menu and party theme. Even if you buy prepared food or have your party catered, give thought to the Ayurvedic balance of the menu, providing all six tastes. Pay attention to detail, balance and surroundings. Provide *churans* for each dosha in a pretty bowl on the table.

Use cloth napkins, rather than paper ones, whenever possible – they don't require a tree to be sacrificed and they make your guests feel honoured. Try to avoid paper plates and disposable plastic utensils.

Surround yourself and your guests with fresh flowers. If you don't want to spend money on flowers, go into nature and respectfully gather wildflowers. Fill bowls with pinecones. Scatter autumn leaves on the table. Nature provides – you just have to receive her beautiful gifts.

The most important aspect of entertaining is the love with which you do it. If you surround yourself and your friends with a harmonious environment, a beautiful table and lovingly prepared food, your party will be a success.

Read more about entertaining in chapter 8, Orchestrating a Feast (page 202).

Chapter

2

How to Eat

Of course, you know how to eat. You've been swallowing things in your mouth even before you hatched as a larva all those years ago. If you could see yourself as a budding human in the womb you'd notice that when you're happy and content, you're swallowing. But if Mum is stressed, you feel anxious, your heart speeds up and your swallowing stops.

Upon our arrival on this planet, we quickly associate the taste of sweet, warm nourishment with the comfort of being close to the woman we love. Ah, the joy and comfort of food in the mouth and food in the belly! At this stage, if we're hungry, we roar loudly a few times and are promptly rewarded with milk on tap.

WHAT WENT WRONG?

As we advance in our independence and begin to suspect that there may actually be someone else out there, we notice that sometimes our hunger needs are not instantly gratified and sometimes the spoon keeps coming at us even when we don't want any more. It's at this point that we may begin to forget what it means to self-refer. By self-referral, we mean the ability to rely upon our own internal signals of comfort and discomfort to regulate our lives. When our tummies are full but the food continues to arrive, we learn not to pay attention to the messages coming from our inner space.

A few years later, when we are able to manipulate the spoon ourselves, we get other messages from our well-intentioned carers. These fall into two main sound bites:

Message #1: 'Finish everything on your plate . . . there are children starving in _____!'

If you were raised in the United States or Britain, it was usually the poor kids in India who were somehow the beneficiaries of your cleaning your plate. Deepak tells us that in his home in New Delhi, he was told that it was the children in China that were going hungry. We suspect that Chinese mums are telling their offspring that they had better finish all their noodles because there are children in Chicago missing meals.

Message #2: 'It's time to eat. Do you think I am running a restaurant?'

As parents, we understand the desire to cook for everyone in the family at the same time and not be at the beck and call of every hungry mouth in the house. However, we all have our own natural rhythms, which may not be completely in sync with everyone else in the household. Although we've all learned from an early age that 'breakfast is the most important meal of the day', for some of us this means eating a four-course feast at

7.00 A.M. and for others it means a croissant and a cup of tea at 10.00 A.M.

We are taught at a very early age not to honour the supreme genius of our bodies. We eat when we are not really hungry 'because it's time to eat'. We don't eat when our bodies are calling for fuel because we are too busy, trying to lose weight or waiting for 'the restaurant to open'. We lose the intimate and delicate connection with our inner wisdom as children and spend the rest of our lives trying to regain it.

The workplace of today is designed for productivity. When we all earned our daily bread by farming the land to grow the wheat to bake in it, it was natural for us to feast on our main meal around noon, relax for an hour or so afterwards and then finish our chores. Today we wolf down a sandwich while talking on the phone over lunch, arrive home in the evening tired and hungry, eat a big meal and go to bed with a full stomach. It's no wonder that so many of us sleep poorly and that functional digestive disorders afflict more than 30 percent of the U.S. population.

BACK TO BASICS

It's not that we don't know how to eat; it's just that we've accepted a few confusing messages that get in the way between our bodies and our minds. This is where the ancient system of health from India known as *Ayurveda* comes to the rescue. Ayurveda is a Sanskrit word that translates as the 'science of life'. Ancient healing systems were not afraid to look at the core issues of being alive, and eating is one of those key components. Basically Ayurveda tells us that the nourishment we get from eating is a result of both the food we take in and our ability to digest it properly. We can have a very healthy diet but if our digestive power is weak, we will not take full advantage of the available nutrition. So how we eat is as important as what we eat. There is an old Ayurvedic expression that says: 'If your digestive power is strong, you can convert poison into nectar, but if your digestive power is weak, you can convert nectar into poison.'

BODY INTELLIGENCE TECHNIQUES (BITS)

These twelve points are the way to ensure that we make the best use of everything that we put into our mouth. We call them Body Intelligence Techniques because they rely on the natural wisdom of the body, which we all have available to us. We've just forgotten them for a while, but being reminded is all it takes to make them lively again in our awareness. Let's review them one by one.

1. **Eat in a settled atmosphere.** We digest the environment through all five of our senses. If we watch a violent TV show while eating dinner, we metabolize all those stress and fear chemicals our bodies produce at the same time we're consuming our food. (We've found that Chinese food, in particular, doesn't mix well with anxious spices.) Better to eat in a quiet, relaxed place with people we love. Joy, comfort and delight are the best seasonings to go with a delicious meal.

2. **Never eat when upset.** Although eating an entire cheesecake by ourselves may seem consoling after a fight with our partner, we recommend waiting a little while before trying to bury emotional pain with a whopping dose of carbohydrate, protein or fat. Using food to feed an emotional need unfortunately (1) doesn't work and (2) gets stored as toxicity. Process emotional upsets openly and honestly, then celebrate your good work by preparing and enjoying a scrumptious feast with a good friend.

3. **Always sit down to eat.** We know we're beginning to sound like your grandmother. Sitting down allows you to put your attention on the delectables on your plate. Attention is what activates everything in this universe. Focusing on your food makes it more nourishing.

4. **Eat only when hungry.** Your appetite is your best friend – listen to it. Think of your hunger as a fuel gauge. Zero is so empty that you are literally starving. Very few Westerners have had this experience. Ten is so full you

can barely move. Most of us have felt like this at least once after a Christmas dinner. We recommend waiting until your appetite is at a 2 or 3 before eating. This means you are really hungry but will survive if you have to wait an hour. Then once you *sit* to eat, go until you are at a 7 – then stop. Seven is the point where you are comfortably full. You could eat more but your hunger is satiated.

5. Reduce ice-cold food and drink. Your taste buds and digestive juices work best at body temperature. The things we tend to take ice cold (fizzy drinks) usually don't taste that good at body temperature so we try to sneak them past our taste buds by first numbing them with ice. Of course, ice cream doesn't do well at 37°C/98.6°F, so we recommend eating this treat at midday when our digestive power is strongest.

6. Don't talk while chewing your food. Attention is empowering. Hear, feel, see, taste and smell each morsel as it enters you. This allows your system to get the greatest nourishment per chew.

7. Eat at a moderate pace. If you pace yourself throughout the meal and remain in present moment awareness, you will never overeat. It's when we're doing other things while eating (watching TV, talking on the phone, balancing the chequebook) that we lose contact with our inner signals. If we are moving really fast, we will probably zoom past level 7 on the appetite gauge and then wonder why we ate that last helping.

8. Eat freshly cooked meals. The Sanskrit word *prana* means 'life force'. The more *prana* we take in, the more vital energy we have available to us. Locally grown, freshly prepared foods carry the highest value of life force. Ideally, the farmer, the supermarket employee and the cook are all happy, loving people so their nourishing life force contributes to the *prana* of the meal.

9. Reduce raw foods. We know that many diets over the years have strongly encouraged the use of raw foods. There is no doubt that overcooking destroys vitamins and other essential nutrients. Properly cooked foods

(1) taste and smell much better and (2) are easier to digest. We invented fire a while ago because, in addition to keeping us warm and scaring away sabre-toothed cats, it made it easier to digest our meals.

10. Experience all six tastes at every meal: *sweet, sour, salty, pungent, bitter and astringent.* These are the six tastes that make the culinary world go round. If all six are represented at each meal, it will be nutritionally balanced and you will feel satisfied after eating it.

11. Leave one-third to one-quarter of your stomach empty. Leaving some space in the stomach makes digestion a lot easier. Pay attention to level 7 on your appetite gauge and you'll have enough room in your belly to digest the scrumptious nourishing fuel.

12. Sit quietly for a few minutes after your meal. Let your attention be in your body for a little while after you eat. A miracle is in process. Packages of energy and information that were outside you just moments ago are being transformed in your body. Eating is a magical, spiritual experience. Savour it for a few moments.

FROZEN, LEFTOVER, UNNATURAL, NUKED, TINNED FOOD

Don't strain. Food is for nourishment. Although we can create a lot of drama around eating, we think it should be easy and joyful. Our recommendation is to use fresh and freshly prepared food *whenever possible.* According to Ayurveda, food provides more than carbohydrates, proteins, fats, vitamins, minerals and trace elements. It also carries intelligence – life force, *prana* – and the fresher the food the more life force is available. Therefore frozen or tinned French beans are not as rich in *prana*, even if they have the same grams of carbohydrates, as beans picked fresh from your garden. However, if you cannot always find the ideal fresh source, don't fret. How you eat is as important as what you eat. If while you are preparing and eating your meal there is joy and love in your heart, the *prana* will be there.

Whenever possible we recommend traditional heat sources for cooking. Microwave ovens were hard to come by five thousand years ago when the ancient Ayurvedic texts were written so they don't have a lot to say about them. Our main contention with microwaves is that they are usually resorted to when we are in a big hurry to heat up frozen or leftover foods, neither of which are terribly rich in *prana*. If you find yourself 'nuking' a lot, it's probably a sign that your life is moving too fast and there's some static in your mind-body connection that needs attention.

VEGETARIANISM

If you eat your vegetables, you'll live longer and be healthier and kinder to your purse and to the earth. A vegetarian diet can be creative, delicious and balanced and provide plenty of protein, vitamins and minerals. Both heart disease and cancer, the two biggest killers in our society, are much less likely in people who don't eat animals. From an ecological perspective, a pound of hamburger requires about sixteen pounds of grain, making the eating of meat costly in terms of global food resources. Finally, there is the issue of karma, in which the taking of life, with its attendant fear and suffering, has its repercussions.

On the other hand, many of our evolutionary ancestors were hunters and we have the biological ability to eat just about anything – animal or vegetable. Our recommendation on this issue is to eat with awareness. Whatever you are allowing into your mind or body, do so consciously and with honour and respect, giving thanks to the source of the nourishment.

Because we are primarily vegetarians ourselves, the recipes in *The Ayurvedic Cookbook* are meatless. For any of the recipes that call for eggs, you can use egg substitutes or replacers, which are available at health food stores. Remember, though, be sure to follow the directions on the packages. Here again, our watchwords are: *Don't strain.* If Aunt Sophie invited us for dinner and served a savoury chicken soup that she had been lovingly preparing all day, we would joyfully eat it because the love in her cooking would provide incomparable nourishment.

FOOD FETISHES

Over the years, many foods have been targeted as the source of a host of health problems. The common problem foods that we hear about at The Chopra Center for Well Being are dairy products, wheat, sugar, sweet fruits, nightshade vegetables, foods with yeast, refined foods, cooked foods and raw foods. We recognize that people can have sensitivities and intolerances for many common food items and that restricting their intake can relieve symptoms.

We think it's important, however, to remember that how we digest what we eat is as important as what we eat. According to Ayurveda, if our digestive power is strong and balanced, we can eat almost anything and get the nourishment we need. If our digestion is weak, even simple foods can cause problems. If certain common foods seem to be creating problems, look into what might be creating the digestive weakness. The need to have dietary restrictions will often vanish when we strengthen our digestive power. Follow the Body Intelligence Techniques (BITS) (page 18) and the whole environment will be seen as a source of nourishment.

Chapter

3

ANCIENT WISDOM, MODERN NEED

Here we are approaching the millennium where we are breaking the genetic code, surfing cyberspace and building space stations to explore the galaxies. What value is there in referring *back* to ancient knowledge from thousands of years ago? It's a good question. Our answer is that the great seers of the past were explorers of *inner* space and brought back a wealth of precious insights that are as valuable today as they were in bygone times. They delved into the field of consciousness, which modern science is now acknowledging as being more fundamental to life than atoms and molecules. We can use this knowledge to help create health and happiness and we are delighted to share this information with you so all aspects of your life can be nourishing.

At The Chopra Center for Well Being we help people enliven their inner healer. To accomplish this, we place a lot of attention on food and nutrition because learning to nourish ourselves is the basis of health and happiness. There are few joys in life greater than enjoying a delicious meal with people we love. This joy is transformed in our bodies into rejuvenating and healing chemical messengers that course through our vessels, communicating this love of life to every cell in our body.

In both the Eastern and Western traditions, food is basic to life and to health. In the Vedas, the ancient wisdom tradition of India, there is the saying 'Food is Brahman (pure potentiality), Brahman is food'. Hippocrates, the father of modern medicine, said, 'Let food be your medicine and medicine be your food.'

Ayurveda, the ancient system of health from India, is the basis of our programmes. Although Ayurveda was first understood in India, its principles are universal and easily translate to our modern Western lifestyle. We don't have to eat Indian food every day to benefit from this wonderful body of knowledge.

According to Ayurveda, each of us inherits a proportion of three basic mind-body principles, called doshas, which create our unique mental and physical characteristics. Most of us have one or two doshas that are most lively in our nature, with the remaining one(s) less significant. The three doshas are known as **Vata, Pitta** and **Kapha.**

If we have mostly **Vata** dosha, we tend to be thin, light and quick in our thoughts and actions. Change is a constant part of our lives. When **Vata** is balanced, we are creative, enthusiastic and lively. But if **Vata** becomes excessive, we may develop anxiety, insomnia or irregular digestion.

If **Pitta** dosha is most lively in our nature, we tend to be muscular, smart and determined. If **Pitta** is balanced, we are warm, intelligent and a good leader. If out of balance, **Pitta** can make us critical, irritable and aggressive.

If we have mostly **Kapha** dosha in our nature, we tend to have a heavier frame, think and move more leisurely, and are stable. When balanced, **Kapha** creates calmness, sweetness and loyalty. When excessive, **Kapha** can cause us to gain weight, be congested and resist healthy change.

Using the principles of Ayurveda, we can identify our mind-body nature and use this understanding to make the most nourishing choices.

Take a few minutes to complete the questionnaire below, rating each statement as to how well it applied to you over the past year.

	not at all	slightly	somewhat	moderately	very
• I tend to think and act quickly.	1	2	3	4	5
• I am lively and enthusiastic by nature.	1	2	3	4	5
• I tend to be thin and rarely gain weight.	1	2	3	4	5
• My daily schedule of eating meals, going to sleep and awakening tends to vary from day to day.	1	2	3	4	5
• Under stress, I tend to worry and become anxious.	1	2	3	4	5
• I speak quickly and am a lively conversationalist.	1	2	3	4	5
• My feet and hands tend to be cool.	1	2	3	4	5
• I tend to have difficulty falling asleep and awaken easily.	1	2	3	4	5
• My digestion tends to be irregular, with frequent gas or bloating.	1	2	3	4	5
• I tend to eat quickly, finishing my meals before others at my table.	1	2	3	4	5

Total for this section (**v**) _____

• My skin is sensitive, sunburns or breaks out easily.	1	2	3	4	5
• I have a tendency towards indigestion or heartburn.	1	2	3	4	5
• I tend to be a perfectionist with a low tolerance for errors.	1	2	3	4	5

- It is not uncommon for me to have more
  than one bowel movement per day.   1   2   3   4   5
- I feel rested with less than eight
  hours of sleep.   1   2   3   4   5
- I think critically, am a good debater
  and can argue a point forcefully.   1   2   3   4   5
- When pressured, I tend to become
  irritable and impatient.   1   2   3   4   5
- If I begin a new project, I tend not to
  stop until I've completed it.   1   2   3   4   5
- I have a strong appetite and can eat
  large quantities of food if I choose.   1   2   3   4   5
- I tend to perform my activities with
  precision and orderliness.   1   2   3   4   5

Total for this section (P) _____

- I am a good listener. I tend to speak
  only when I feel that I have
  something important to say.   1   2   3   4   5
- I have a tendency to have chronic
  sinus congestion, asthma
  or excessive phlegm.   1   2   3   4   5
- I have a slow digestion and tend
  to feel heavy after eating.   1   2   3   4   5
- I tend to eat slowly.   1   2   3   4   5
- My skin is usually soft and smooth.   1   2   3   4   5
- I tend to perform activities in a
  slow-paced manner.   1   2   3   4   5
- I tend to be loyal and devoted
  in my relationships.   1   2   3   4   5

- I tend to gain weight easily and
  have difficulty losing extra pounds.   1   2   3   4   5

- I tend to be steady and methodical,
  with consistent energy and endurance. 1   2   3   4   5

- I tend to be calm by nature and
  seldom lose my temper.   1   2   3   4   5

Total for this section (K) _____

V_____ P_____ K_____

Now add up the scores for each of the three sections that correspond to
Vata, Pitta and **Kapha.** Rank the three doshas from highest to lowest in
your nature. The dosha that scores the highest is usually the one that needs
to be balanced.

Every wisp of experience that we have influences the balance of doshas
in our mind-body constitution. If we listen to fast-paced, rock and roll
music, it will increase **Vata** and decrease **Kapha.** A sweet Brahms lullaby
will have the opposite effect. For each of the five senses, every experience
can be classified by how it affects each of the doshas.

CREATING BALANCE THROUGH THE SENSES

SENSE OF SMELL

	BALANCES THE DOSHA
VATA	Floral, fruity, warm, sweet, sour aromas – *basil, bergamot, patchouli, vanilla*
PITTA	Cool and sweet aromas – *sandalwood, mint, rose, jasmine*
KAPHA	Stimulating, spicy, aromatic aromas – *eucalyptus, musk, camphor, juniper, clove*

SENSE OF SIGHT

	BALANCES THE DOSHA
VATA	Quiet, peaceful scenery – *blue, gold colours*
PITTA	Cool, soothing scenery *blue, green colours*
KAPHA	Stimulating, lively scenery *red, orange colours*

SENSE OF TOUCH

	BALANCES THE DOSHA
VATA	Gentle, nurturing massage *with sesame or almond oil*
PITTA	Slow, moderate pressure massage *with coconut or olive oil*
KAPHA	Deep stimulating massage *with sesame or mustard oil*

SENSE OF HEARING

	BALANCES THE DOSHA
VATA	Slow-paced, gentle, relaxing rhythms and melodies
PITTA	Medium-paced, sweet, soothing, calming rhythms and melodies
KAPHA	Quick-paced, invigorating, energizing rhythms and melodies

SENSE OF TASTE

When talking about food, the sense of taste is what it's all about. How things taste is how we discovered what was yummy and what was yucky in the first place. Animals and our early human ancestors continually sampled the surrounding scenery, and if it was pleasing to the tongue, it was a pretty safe sign that more could be consumed. If the flavour of the dangling sphere wrapped in its crimson skin was mouthwateringly sweet, we took this as a sign from Mother Nature that the fruit was edible. If the leaf on a bush was intensely bitter, we tended not to add too much of it to our salad for the day.

The word for taste in Ayurveda is *rasa*. It's an interesting word that also means 'emotion' and 'sap'. *Rasa* recognizes that how something tastes in our mouth affects our moods and influences our sense of well-being at subtle levels.

Six tastes are described in Ayurveda:

Sweet   Sour   Salty   Pungent   Bitter   Astringent

We like **sweet** tastes. You don't have to encourage a tot to eat something sugary. But here, sweet is more than just the flavour of sweeteners; it is any food that is mostly carbohydrate, protein or fat. So sweet includes pastas, breads, nuts and meat.

Sour taste adds zest to other flavours. We find it most often in citrus fruits and tomatoes, but it is also present in cheeses, salad dressings and any aged or fermented food.

Salty taste stimulates digestion and makes our mouths water. We use it most in the form of table salt (sodium chloride), but it is also present in soy sauce, tamari and a variety of vegetable seasoning blends.

Pungent taste is the hot spicy flavour that comes from chillies and peppers. Although in some cultures (Mexican and Indian, for example) it's a big part of every meal, most of us like just a taste of it to wake up our lazy taste buds.

Bitter taste is the flavour of green, leafy vegetables. It is also found in tea, coffee and real chocolate. We like bitter in smaller quantities and almost always need to blend other flavours in with it. It tends to be depleting and detoxifying. Most medicinal herbs are bitter.

Astringent taste is really more of a sensation on the tongue and in the mouth. Foods that are astringent make you pucker. Beans and lentils are our major source of the astringent taste. Tea also has this quality. We're ensuring a good source of vegetable protein in our diet when we include the astringent taste of legumes.

Body Intelligence Technique No. 10 says to have all six tastes present at every meal. If each taste is blended into the symphony of flavours, (1) the food will be delicious, (2) you will feel satisfied when you've finished eating and (3) the meal will be nutritionally balanced and complete.

THE SIX TASTES AND MIND-BODY BALANCE

Like every other sense, taste influences the doshas. Three tastes increase and three tastes decrease each dosha.

MIND-BODY PRINCIPLE	TASTES THAT INCREASE	TASTES THAT DECREASE
VATA	Pungent, Bitter, Astringent	Sweet, Sour, Salty
PITTA	Pungent, Sour, Salty	Sweet, Bitter, Astringent
KAPHA	Sweet, Sour, Salty	Pungent, Bitter, Astringent

Depending upon which mind-body principle is most prominent in your nature, you may wish to favour foods that are balancing (reducing) to that dosha. So if you are a **Vata** type and having a spell when you're feeling more anxious and having trouble sleeping, you might create meals that have more sweet, sour and salty tastes with fewer pungent, bitter and astringent flavours. On the other hand, if **Kapha** is dominating, you would favour the pungent, bitter and astringent foods (more leafy vegetables and beans) and back off on the sweet flavours (pastas and breads). This doesn't mean to avoid any taste altogether – it just means to shift the balance.

Below is a catalogue of which foods to favour or reduce for each mind-body type. We can't overemphasize that this doesn't mean getting compulsive about it! Just have the principles in your awareness and listen to your inner messages. If your list says to increase Brussels sprouts and you just hate those little cabbages, then go with your internal signals and find something you like.

Each recipe in this book is categorized according to its influence on the doshas. To emphasize that we are not into straining austerity, the choices for each mind-body type are: less, some, or more. If you are a **Pitta** type and the recipe is *less* for **Pitta,** this means that you should reduce the helping you take of this dish versus another dish that is rated *more* for **Pitta. Some** means use your judgement. If you are cooking for people with a variety of mind-body types, you don't have to prepare three different meals. The mouths you are feeding simply take more of some dishes and less of others. It's really easy, and remember, eating is a *celebration!*

VATA-BALANCING DIET

Vata is drying, cooling and light, so favour foods that are oily, warming and heavy in quality. The best tastes to pacify or balance **Vata** are **sweet, sour** and **salty.** Take less of foods that are pungent, bitter and astringent.

RECOMMENDATIONS

1. To balance the lightness of **Vata** eat larger quantities, but do not overeat.

2. Dairy products pacify **Vata.** Boil milk before drinking it and take it warm.

3. All sweeteners pacify **Vata** and may be taken in moderation.

4. Fats and oils reduce **Vata.**

5. Rice and wheat are the best grains. Reduce the amount of barley, sweetcorn, millet, buckwheat, rye and oats.

6. Favour sweet, heavy fruits such as avocados, bananas, berries, cherries, grapes, mangoes, sweet oranges, papayas, peaches, pineapples and plums. Reduce dry or light fruits like apples, cranberries, pears and pomegranates.

7. Cooked vegetables are best. Raw vegetables should be minimized. Favour asparagus, beetroot and carrots. Other vegetables, such as peas, broccoli, cauliflower, courgettes and potatoes, may be taken in moderation if well cooked in ghee (clarified butter) or oil. Sprouts and cabbage tend to produce gas and should be minimized.

8. Spices known to pacify **Vata** are cardamom, cumin, ginger, cinnamon, salt, cloves, mustard seed and black pepper. **Vata** *churans* are also useful.

9. All varieties of nuts are recommended.

10. Except for tofu and mung dhal, reduce the intake of beans.

11. For nonvegetarians, chicken, turkey and seafood are best; beef should be minimized.

LIGHTER VATA-BALANCING DIET

Although oily, heavier, sweeter and richer foods are usually recommended to pacify **Vata,** sometimes lighter foods with **Vata**-pacifying qualities are desirable. For example, if you find yourself overeating out of nervousness or anxiety, a *lighter* **Vata** diet will help to settle your mind without adding pounds to your body.

RECOMMENDATIONS

1. Rice, wheat and oats, prepared with reduced amounts of oil or sweeteners, are the favoured grains.

2. All sweeteners may be taken in *reduced* amounts.

3. Favour low-fat milk and lassi. Reduce your quantities of cheese and cream.

4. All oils except for coconut can be used in small quantities. *Small* amounts of ghee may be taken.

5. Green or yellow mung beans and red lentils are preferable. They are usually prepared by mixing one part dried beans with two parts water and boiling to the consistency of soup.

6. Vegetables should be well cooked and are best taken in soups, casseroles and stews. Almost all vegetables are acceptable, with carrots, courgettes, asparagus, spinach, tomato and artichoke most desirable.

7. Favour sweet, ripe fruits in season. Figs, pineapples, grapes, apricots, sweet oranges, papayas and small amounts of raisins are acceptable.

8. The warmer and sweeter spices are useful, including ginger, cumin, cinnamon, cardamom, fennel, cloves, asafoetida (hing) and anise. Salt, lemon juice and tamarind are also fine in small amounts.

PITTA-BALANCING DIET

Pitta dosha can overheat the mind and body, so favour cool foods and liquids. Foods with **sweet, bitter** and **astringent** tastes are best. Reduce foods that are pungent, salty and sour.

RECOMMENDATIONS

1. To balance the heat of **Pitta,** take milk, butter and ghee. Use less yoghurt, cheese, sour cream and buttermilk, as the sour taste aggravates **Pitta.**

2. All sweeteners, except treacle and honey, may be taken in moderation.

3. Olive, sunflower and coconut oils are best to pacify **Pitta.** Use less sesame, almond and corn oil, which are more heating.

4. Wheat, rice, barley and oats are the best grains to reduce **Pitta.** Use less corn, rye, millet and brown rice.

5. Sweeter fruits, such as grapes, melons, cherries, coconuts, avocados, mangoes, pomegranates, and fully ripe pineapples, oranges and plums, are recommended. Reduce sour fruits, such as grapefruits, apricots and berries.

6. Vegetables to favour are asparagus, cucumbers, potatoes, sweet potatoes, green leafy vegetables, pumpkins, broccoli, cauliflower, celery, okra, lettuce, green beans and courgettes. Reduce tomatoes, hot peppers, carrots, beetroot, aubergine, onions, garlic, radishes and spinach.

7. **Pitta** types need to use seasonings that are more soothing and cooling. These include cinnamon, coriander, cardamom and fennel. Hotter spices such as ginger, cumin, black pepper, fenugreek, clove, salt and mustard seed should be used sparingly. Very hot seasonings such as chilli peppers and cayenne are best avoided. **Pitta** *churans* are also useful.

8. For non-vegetarians, chicken, pheasant and turkey are preferable; beef, seafood and eggs increase **Pitta** and should be minimized.

KAPHA-BALANCING DIET

Kapha dosha is heavy, oily and cold, so favour foods that are light, dry and warm. Foods with **pungent, bitter** and **astringent** tastes are most beneficial for pacifying **Kapha.** Reduce foods with sweet, sour and salty tastes.

RECOMMENDATIONS

1. Dairy products tend to increase **Kapha** so low-fat milk is best. Boiling milk before drinking it makes it easier to digest. Adding turmeric or ginger to milk before boiling reduces its **Kapha**-increasing qualities.

2. Apples and pears, which are considered lighter fruits, are recommended. Reduce heavier fruits like bananas, avocados, coconuts, melons, dates, figs or sour oranges.

3. Honey is a sweetener that is said to pacify **Kapha.** Other sweeteners increase **Kapha** and should be reduced.

4. All beans, except for soya beans and tofu, are good for **Kapha** types.

5. Favour the grains of barley, sweetcorn, millet, buckwheat, rye and oats. Reduce the intake of rice and wheat.

6. Reduce all nuts.

7. All spices except salt are pacifying to **Kapha. Kapha** *churans* are also useful.

8. All vegetables except for tomatoes, cucumbers, sweet potatoes and courgettes are suitable for **Kapha** types.

9. For non-vegetarians, white chicken meat, turkey and seafood are acceptable. Reduce the intake of red meats.

MAKING IT REALLY EASY — CHURANS OR HERBAL/SPICE BLENDS

The mystery and magic of cooking is in the spicing. Just as every food influences each mind-body principle, so does every herb and spice. Blends of dosha-balancing seasonings are available or can be prepared to be used in cooking or sprinkled on food during a meal. These herb and spice blends (*churans*) ensure that each taste is represented in the right proportion. **Vata, Pitta** and **Kapha** types eating the same pasta primavera can use the appropriate *churan* to personalize their meal.

ABOUT DIETING

Nature expresses her creativity in the variety of shapes and forms that we cherish in the world around us. In our appreciation for the wisdom of nature, we honour the uniqueness of each human being. A daffodil has a different size, shape and colour from an iris and we can appreciate the beauty of both. The idea that we all need to strive for an idealized 'perfect' body contrasts with our understanding that nature intentionally and lovingly creates diversity. Nutritional programmes that deprive you of food, require strict calorie counting or recommend prolonged use of synthesized, liquefied substances do not enhance balance and can rarely be sustained. For those of you who wish to shed unwanted pounds, we recommend eating consciously using the Body Intelligence Techniques (BITS) (page 18), following an exercise programme appropriate to your mind-body type, and reducing the amount of fat in your diet while following a dosha-balancing regimen.

Many of the recipes in *The Ayurvedic Cookbook* are naturally low in fat and/or calories and are marked with a heart ♥. Favouring these recipes will help you to realize your weight loss goals while allowing you to participate fully in the celebration of nourishment.

Chapter
4

RECIPES FOR
NUTRITIONAL BLISS

Regardless of your predominant dosha you can enjoy
each one of these recipes. Ayurveda is not a system of
restriction but rather one that focuses on balance. For
each recipe, the main tastes are listed and a recommendation is made regarding the quantity that should be consumed based upon your dosha. For example, if you are a
Kapha type and a recipe suggests that you take less of that
dish, this does not mean you have to avoid it altogether. It
simply means that on a relative basis, other dishes that are
more pacifying to **Kapha** should be taken in greater quantity. If two doshas are fairly equally represented in your
physiology, favour foods that are balancing to both of
those doshas. Again, we cannot emphasize enough that
eating with awareness ensures that the quality and quantity of the food you consume will provide the ideal nourishment for your mind and body.

Starters and Snacks

◆

Starters should tease the appetite, not fill the tummy. When serving starters, remember to bring them to room temperature or slightly warm them (cold food before a meal kills *agni,* or digestive fire). Think of the balance and general tastes of your meal when planning a menu with starters.

Snacks are often satisfying enough for an evening meal when balanced and filling. Chutneys enhance the flavours of many snack items, so be sure to look into Condiments and Beverages (page 162) for preparation.

ASIAN EGGS

BABA GHANOUJ

BLACK BEAN DIP

CRANBERRY BLISS
BALLS

BRUSCHETTA

CHILLI CHICKPEAS

CURRIED COCONUT
ALMONDS

GUACAMOLE AND
CHAPATTI SNACKS

HUMMUS DIP

HUMMUS DIP, THAI
STYLE

SHAKTI DATE BALLS

RICE AND PEAS
SNACK

SAVOURY TORTE

ZIPPY ALMONDS

ᗩSIAN ᕮGGS

◆

These delicate eggs are spicy and sweet.

25 minutes to prepare

12 hard-boiled eggs *(sweet)*
1 tablespoon unsalted butter *(sweet)*
2 tablespoons sesame seeds *(sweet)*
½ teaspoon cumin *(pungent)*

2 pinches garam masala *(pungent)*
2 pinches turmeric *(bitter, pungent, astringent)*

1. Slice the eggs in half lengthways.
2. Heat the butter in a frying pan. Add the sesame seeds and spices and cook for 30 seconds.
3. Carefully place the eggs, cut sides down, in the frying pan. Cook for 2 minutes. Turn the eggs over carefully so they don't come apart. Cook for 2 more minutes.
4. Serve warm or at room temperature.

Serves 6

Prominent Tastes: *Sweet, Pungent*	
If you want to reduce	*eat*
VATA	MORE
PITTA	SOME
KAPHA	LESS

Baba Ghanouj

◆

Serve this with wholemeal pitta bread.

45 minutes to prepare

1 large aubergine, peeled and cut into strips *(bitter)*

110g/4oz sesame tahini *(sweet)*

Juice of 1 lemon *(sour, astringent)*

1 teaspoon soy sauce *(astringent, salty)*

1 garlic clove, minced *(all but sour)*

Paprika, to taste *(pungent)*

1 teaspoon olive oil *(sweet)*

1 teaspoon chopped fresh mint or coriander *(pungent)*

1. Preheat the oven to 180°C/350°F/gas mark 4.
2. Place the aubergine strips in a baking dish in the oven for approximately 30 minutes, or until soft and tender. Reserve the liquid. Cool the aubergine completely and place in a food processor with all the remaining ingredients, including the reserved liquid. (For very different tastes, choose either mint or coriander.) Blend well.
3. Refrigerate until 1 hour before serving.

Serves 6 to 8

Prominent Tastes: *Bitter, Pungent, Sweet*	
If you want to reduce	eat
VATA	LESS
PITTA	MORE
KAPHA	SOME

♥Black Bean Dip
◆

This dip can be made ahead by soaking the beans one day, cooking the next and preparing the day of the party. It goes well with Guacamole and Chapatti Snacks (page 46).

20 minutes to prepare (not including time to cook beans)

200g/7oz dry black beans *(sweet, astringent)*

1 garlic clove, minced *(all but sour)*

1 teaspoon vegetable bouillon powder *(all)*

1 teaspoon cumin *(pungent)*

1 teaspoon soy sauce *(astringent, salty)*

2 tablespoons minced spring onions or 1 tablespoon dried minced onion *(pungent)*

2 tablespoons minced fresh coriander *(pungent)*

1. Soak the beans overnight in 700 ml/1¼ pints of water. In the morning, drain and rinse the beans well to remove any foam. Place in a pot with another 700ml/1¼ pints of water and bring to a boil. Reduce to a simmer and cook until the beans are quite tender, about 2 hours, adding more water if necessary. Be sure to skim off any foam that rises to the top while cooking; this reduces the flatulent character of the beans. Cool to room temperature.
2. Mash well and blend with the remaining ingredients. If the dip is too thick, add a little more water to give it a good dipping consistency.
3. Refrigerate until 1 hour before serving.

Serves 6 to 8

Prominent Tastes: *Sweet, Pungent, Astringent*	
If you want to reduce	*eat*
VATA	SOME
PITTA	LESS
KAPHA	SOME

CRANBERRY BLISS BALLS

◆

These little yummies are a favourite energy source for between meals or as a light dessert.

20 minutes to prepare

170g/6oz dried cranberries *(sweet)*
60g/2oz pine nuts *(sweet)*
40g/1½oz desiccated coconut plus 30g/1oz coconut, for rolling *(sweet)*

30g/1oz sunflower seeds *(sweet, bitter)*
2 teaspoons maple syrup *(sweet)*

1. Place the cranberries and pine nuts in a food processor. Process for about 1 minute. Pour in the 40g/1½oz coconut, sunflower seeds and maple syrup and process for an additional 20 seconds.
2. Scoop out 1 teaspoon at a time, form into balls, and roll in the remaining coconut. Refrigerate for at least 30 minutes to firm the balls.
3. These can be stored in an airtight container in the refrigerator.

Serves 12

Prominent Taste: *Sweet*	
If you want to reduce	*eat*
VATA	MORE
PITTA	SOME
KAPHA	LESS

♥Bruschetta

◆

Make this in summer with tomatoes right off the vine.

20 minutes to prepare

Bruschetta Topping

450g/1 lb fresh, vine-ripened plum
tomatoes, chopped and drained
(sweet, sour)

1 garlic clove, minced *(all but sour)*

1 tablespoon minced spring onions
(pungent, sweet)

1 teaspoon lemon zest *(bitter)*

Juice of 1 lemon *(sour, astringent)*

8 slices of bread or 1 recipe
Focaccia (page 132) *(sweet)*

60ml/2 fl oz olive oil, optional
(sweet)

40g/1½oz minced fresh basil
(pungent)

1. Blend the bruschetta topping ingredients in a small bowl. Refrigerate
   until 1 hour before serving.
2. Toast the bread or make the focaccia, brushing with olive oil, if desired,
   before toasting or baking.
3. Add the fresh basil to the topping mixture just before serving.
4. Serve the warm toast or focaccia with bowls of the bruschetta topping.

Serves 6 to 8

Prominent Tastes: *Sweet, Pungent, Astringent*	
If you want to reduce	*eat*
VATA	MORE
PITTA	LESS
KAPHA	MORE

♥Chilli Chickpeas

•

Serve this quick, spicy filling with chapattis or pitta bread for a snack, lunch or dinner.

20 minutes to prepare

400g/14oz cooked chickpeas, drained *(sweet, astringent)*

1 tablespoon Thai-style chilli paste *(pungent)*

¼ teaspoon lemon grass *(pungent, sour)*

1 tablespoon soy sauce *(astringent, salty)*

60ml/2 fl oz coconut milk *(sweet)*

2 tablespoons finely chopped fresh coriander *(pungent)*

1. Heat a small frying pan over medium heat. Add the chickpeas, chilli paste, lemon grass and soy sauce. Stir frequently. Cook until the chilli paste is melted and the chickpeas begin to brown, about 10 minutes.
2. Add the coconut milk and cook an additional 5 minutes, until somewhat thickened. Remove from heat.
3. Toss with the coriander just before serving.

Serves 4 to 8

Prominent Tastes: *Sweet, Pungent*	
If you want to reduce	*eat*
VATA	SOME
PITTA	LESS
KAPHA	MORE

CURRIED COCONUT ALMONDS

◆

Almonds are sweet and slightly bitter. Soaking them overnight increases their digestibility.

20 minutes to prepare

½ teaspoon ghee or olive oil *(sweet)*

300g/10oz whole almonds, soaked overnight and dried *(sweet, bitter)*

1 garlic clove, minced or crushed *(all but sour)*

1 teaspoon soy sauce *(astringent, salty)*

1 teaspoon crushed chillies or ½ teaspoon chilli paste *(pungent)*

¼ teaspoon turmeric *(pungent)*

¼ teaspoon ground ginger *(pungent, sweet)*

¼ teaspoon cinnamon *(pungent, bitter)*

¼ teaspoon cardamom *(pungent, sweet)*

¼ teaspoon cumin *(pungent)*

1 teaspoon natural (unrefined) sugar *(sweet)*

30g/1oz dried toasted coconut *(sweet)*

1. In a frying pan, heat the ghee or oil to the smoking point. Sauté the almonds in the medium-hot ghee or oil for 5 minutes, stirring frequently. Add the garlic, soy sauce, chillies or chilli paste, spices and sugar. Toss with the toasted coconut.
2. Turn off the heat. Let stand for 10 minutes, or until completely cooled.
3. These may be stored in an airtight container for 6 weeks.

Serves 8 to 12

Prominent Tastes: *Sweet, Bitter, Pungent*	
If you want to reduce	*eat*
VATA	MORE
PITTA	SOME
KAPHA	LESS

♥Guacamole and Chapatti Snacks
◆

This variation on a traditional Mexican dish is low in fat because the bread is baked, not fried.

25 minutes to prepare

Guacamole

3 ripe avocados, mashed *(sweet)*

2 spring onions, minced *(pungent, sweet)*

2 tablespoons minced fresh coriander *(pungent)*

Juice of 2 limes *(sour)*

1 teaspoon soy sauce *(astringent, salty)*

60g/2oz low-fat plain yoghurt *(sweet, sour)*

Coriander sprigs *(pungent)*

6 wholemeal Chapattis (page 146), cut into strips *(sweet)*

Salt *(salty)*

1. Blend the guacamole ingredients in a small bowl. Garnish with the coriander sprigs.
2. Brush the chapatti strips with warm salted water and place on racks set on baking dishes in a very hot (240°C/475°F/gas mark 9) oven for about 10 minutes, or until lightly browned.
3. Serve with the guacamole.

Serves 8 to 12

Prominent Tastes: *Sweet, Pungent, Sour*	
If you want to reduce	*eat*
VATA	MORE
PITTA	SOME
KAPHA	LESS

❤Hummus Dip

❖

Our version of Middle Eastern hummus has no added oil, saving masses of calories. Serve this with wholemeal pitta bread.

20 minutes to prepare

600g/1 lb 5oz cooked chickpeas *(sweet, astringent)*

60g/2oz sesame tahini *(sweet)*

Juice of 1 lemon *(sour, astringent)*

60–110ml/2–4 fl oz orange juice (organic orange juice concentrate may be used for a more intense flavour) *(sweet, sour)*

1 teaspoon soy sauce *(astringent, salty)*

1 garlic clove, minced *(all but sour)*

Paprika, to taste *(pungent)*

1 teaspoon chopped fresh coriander *(pungent)*

1. Place the chickpeas in a food processor and process for 3 minutes, until smooth. Water may be added if the paste becomes too thick to mix. Add the remaining ingredients and process until smooth.
2. Refrigerate until 1 hour before serving.

Serves 8 to 12

Prominent Tastes: *Sweet, Astringent*	
If you want to reduce	*eat*
VATA	SOME
PITTA	SOME
KAPHA	SOME

♥Hummus Dip, Thai Style

◆

A touch of Thai chilli paste adds a new dimension to hummus.
Serve this with wholemeal pitta bread.

20 minutes to prepare

600g/1 lb 5oz cooked chickpeas *(sweet, astringent)*

60ml/2 fl oz coconut milk *(sweet)*

Juice of 1 lemon *(sour, astringent)*

60–110ml/2–4 fl oz orange juice (organic orange juice concentrate may be used for more intense flavour) *(sweet, sour)*

1 teaspoon soy sauce *(astringent, salty)*

1 garlic clove, minced *(all but sour)*

1 to 2 teaspoons Thai chilli paste *(pungent)*

1 teaspoon chopped fresh coriander *(pungent)*

1. Place the chickpeas in a food processor and process for 3 minutes, until smooth. Water may be added if the paste becomes too thick to mix. Add the remaining ingredients and process until smooth.
2. Refrigerate until 1 hour before serving.

Serves 8 to 12

Prominent Tastes: *Sweet, Pungent, Astringent*	
If you want to reduce	eat
VATA	SOME
PITTA	SOME
KAPHA	SOME

Shakti Date Balls

◆

Here's another high-energy snack.

10 minutes to prepare

170g/6oz dried date pieces *(sweet)*

60g/2oz walnuts *(sweet)*

40g/1½oz desiccated coconut *(sweet)*

30g/1oz sunflower seeds *(sweet, bitter)*

2 teaspoons honey *(sweet)*

30g/1oz toasted sesame seeds, for rolling *(sweet)*

1. Place the dates, walnuts, coconut and sunflower seeds in a food processor. Process for about 1 minute, until well chopped but not pulverized. Pour in the honey and process for an additional 20 seconds.
2. Scoop out 1 teaspoon at a time, form into balls, and roll in sesame seeds. Refrigerate for at least 30 minutes to firm the balls.
3. These can be stored in an airtight container in the refrigerator.

Serves 4 to 6

Prominent Taste: *Sweet*	
If you want to reduce	eat
VATA	MORE
PITTA	SOME
KAPHA	LESS

♥Rice and Peas Snack

•

5 minutes to prepare

140g/5oz cooked basmati rice (*sweet*)

90g/3oz cooked fresh or frozen organic peas (*sweet, astringent*)

1 tablespoon currants (*sweet*)

1 teaspoon soy sauce (*astringent, salty*)

1 teaspoon lemon juice (*sour, astringent*)

Pinch of grated nutmeg (*pungent, astringent*)

1 teaspoon ghee (optional) (*sweet*)

Toss all the ingredients together.

Serves 4 to 6

Prominent Taste: *Sweet*	
If you want to reduce	eat
VATA	MORE
PITTA	SOME
KAPHA	SOME

Savoury Torte

◆

Here's a quick, delicious first course using a quick, frozen speciality. This is one of those times when frozen is much preferred to making your own pastry dough, since making your own would increase the time by about 3 hours! Make sure your other ingredients are fresh, fresh, fresh.

45 minutes to prepare

500g/17¾oz frozen puff pastry *(sweet)*

4 red onions *(pungent)*

½ teaspoon ghee *(sweet)*

1 yellow pepper *(pungent)*

110g/4oz chèvre goat cheese *(sweet)*

170g/6oz chopped sun-dried tomatoes *(sour)*

¼ teaspoon fresh rosemary *(pungent, bitter)*

30g/1oz grated Parmesan cheese *(sweet)*

1. Follow the directions on the packet of puff pastry for thawing and rolling out.
2. In a frying pan, sauté the onions in the ghee until well browned and caramelized, about 20 minutes. Set aside to cool.
3. Roast the yellow pepper over a gas or electric hob or in the oven. Cool. Peel the skin away by rubbing between your fingers. Chop the pepper well.
4. Preheat the oven to 200°C/400°F/gas mark 6.
5. Arrange the pastry on a large oiled baking tray, crimping the edges to form a ridge. Spread the chèvre over the surface, then sprinkle all the remaining ingredients over the top, ending with the Parmesan cheese.
6. Bake for 25 minutes, or until the pastry is golden. Serve warm or at room temperature.

Serves 4 to 8

Prominent Tastes: *Sweet, Pungent*	
If you want to reduce	*eat*
VATA	MORE
PITTA	LESS
KAPHA	SOME

Zippy Almonds

◆

*Almonds are sweet and slightly bitter. Soaking them overnight
increases their digestibility. These almonds have a spicy, fiery
flavour – great to boost the appetite.*

20 minutes to prepare

½ teaspoon ghee or olive oil *(sweet)*

150g/5oz whole almonds, soaked
overnight and dried *(sweet, bitter)*

1 garlic clove, minced or crushed
(all but sour)

1 teaspoon soy sauce *(astringent,
salty)*

1 teaspoon crushed chillies or
½ teaspoon chilli paste *(pungent)*

1 teaspoon natural (unrefined)
sugar *(sweet)*

1. Heat the ghee or oil to the smoking point in a frying pan. Sauté the
   almonds in medium-hot ghee or oil for 5 minutes, stirring frequently.
   Add the garlic, soy sauce, chillies or chilli paste and sugar. Toss to coat
   the almonds.
2. Turn off the heat and let stand for 10 minutes, or until completely
   cooled.
3. These may be stored in an airtight container for 6 weeks.

Serves 8 to 12

Prominent Tastes: *Sweet, Bitter, Pungent*	
If you want to reduce	*eat*
VATA	MORE
PITTA	LESS
KAPHA	LESS

Soups

◆

Regardless of the season, a great soup is always appreciated. Organic vegetable bouillon, or broth powders are useful to save time, but fresh stocks are always a wonderful contribution to the flavour and nutrition of soup.

ACORN SQUASH SOUP	WINTER SQUASH SOUP
CURRIED CARROT SOUP	RED LENTIL DHAL
GREEN SPLIT PEA DHAL	SPINACH SOUP
MUNG BEAN KITCHARI	WATERMELON SOUP
POTATO-LEEK SOUP	*(with Beetroot and Orange)*

❤Acorn Squash Soup
◆

This soup is creamy without cream.

1¹/₂ hours to prepare

6 medium acorn squash, cut into quarters *(sweet)*

950ml/1¾ pints vegetable stock *(all)*

3 tablespoons vegetable bouillon powder *(all)*

2 tablespoons soy sauce *(astringent, salty)*

¼ teaspoon sea salt *(salty)*

1 tablespoon cinnamon *(pungent, bitter)*

½ teaspoon cloves *(pungent)*

½ teaspoon ground ginger *(pungent, sweet)*

1. Place the squash, cut side down, on an oiled or sprayed baking sheet, cover with foil, and bake 45 minutes in a 190°C/375°F/gas mark 5 oven. Cool.
2. Scoop the pulp from the squash and combine with the vegetable stock, vegetable bouillon powder, soy sauce, salt, cinnamon, cloves and ginger in a large saucepan. Simmer for about 20 minutes. With a hand-held soup blender, mash the pulp to blend well with the stock.
3. Add a scoop of yoghurt before serving warm or slightly chilled.

Serves 4 to 6

Prominent Tastes: *Sweet, Pungent*	
If you want to reduce	*eat*
VATA	MORE
PITTA	SOME
KAPHA	SOME

♥Curried Carrot Soup

◆

A light touch of curry gives this carrot soup a tangy zip.

30 minutes to prepare

½ teaspoon olive oil or ghee *(sweet)*

8 medium carrots, cut into pieces *(sweet, pungent)*

½ yellow onion, diced *(pungent, sweet)*

2 tablespoons vegetable bouillon powder *(all)*

2 tablespoons soy sauce *(astringent, salty)*

¼ teaspoon sea salt *(salty)*

1 teaspoon cinnamon *(pungent, bitter)*

½ teaspoon turmeric *(bitter, pungent, astringent)*

½ teaspoon cardamom *(pungent, sweet)*

¼ teaspoon crushed chillies *(pungent)*

½ teaspoon ground cloves *(pungent)*

½ teaspoon ground ginger *(pungent, sweet)*

1. Heat the oil or ghee in a large saucepan to the smoking point. Sauté the carrots and onion in the oil or ghee for 5 minutes, stirring frequently. Cover with 950 ml/1¾ pints of water, bring to a boil and cook for 20 minutes.
2. Add the remaining ingredients. With a hand-held soup blender, process until smooth.
3. Simmer for 10 minutes. Serve warm.

Serves 4 to 6

Prominent Tastes: *Sweet, Pungent*	
If you want to reduce	*eat*
VATA	MORE
PITTA	SOME
KAPHA	MORE

♥ Green Split Pea Dhal

◆

Split peas are a reminder of Mum, home and hearth.

2½ hours to prepare (not including time to soak beans)

230g/8oz dried green split peas
(sweet, astringent)

Pinch of sea salt (salty)

110g/4oz diced carrots (sweet,
pungent)

1 celery stalk, diced (bitter,
astringent)

3 tablespoons vegetable bouillon
powder (all)

1 teaspoon ghee (sweet)

1 tablespoon mustard seeds
(pungent)

1 teaspoon ground coriander
(pungent, bitter)

1 teaspoon turmeric (bitter,
pungent, astringent)

2.5cm/1in piece of fresh root
ginger, grated, or 1 teaspoon
ground ginger (pungent, sweet)

1 teaspoon cumin (pungent)

2 tablespoons soy sauce (astringent,
salty)

1. In a large saucepan, soak the peas in 950 ml/1¾ pints of water overnight. Drain and rinse well. Add 950 ml/1¾ pints of water, the salt, carrots, celery and vegetable bouillon powder. Simmer over low heat for about 2 hours, until tender.

2. In a frying pan, heat the ghee to the smoking point. Add the mustard seeds. When they begin to sputter and pop, add to the peas with the remaining ingredients. Simmer over low heat for about 15 minutes.

Serves 6 to 8

Prominent Tastes: *Pungent, Astringent*	
If you want to reduce	eat
VATA	LESS
PITTA	SOME
KAPHA	SOME

♥Winter Squash Soup
♦

This smooth autumn soup has a delicious aroma.

1¹/₂ hours to prepare

6 gem squash, cut into quarters *(sweet)*

950ml/1¾ pints vegetable stock *(all)*

3 tablespoons vegetable bouillon powder *(all)*

2 tablespoons soy sauce *(astringent, salty)*

¼ teaspoon sea salt *(salty)*

1 tablespoon cinnamon *(pungent, bitter)*

½ teaspoon cloves *(pungent)*

½ teaspoon ground ginger *(pungent, sweet)*

400ml/14 fl oz coconut milk *(sweet)*

Low-fat plain yoghurt *(sweet, sour)*

1. Place the squash on a lightly oiled baking sheet, cover with foil and bake 45 minutes in a 190°C/375° F/gas mark 5 oven. Cool.
2. Scoop the pulp from the squash. Combine with the remaining ingredients except the yoghurt in a large saucepan. Simmer for about 20 minutes. With a hand-held soup blender, mash the pulp to blend well with the stock.
3. Add a scoop of yoghurt before serving.

Serves 4 to 6

Prominent Tastes: *Sweet, Pungent, Astringent*	
If you want to reduce	*eat*
VATA	MORE
PITTA	SOME
KAPHA	SOME

❤Red Lentil Dhal
◆

Red lentils turn slightly green when cooked.
They cook more quickly than brown or green lentils.

1½ hours to prepare

230g/8oz dried red lentils *(sweet, astringent)*

Pinch of sea salt *(salty)*

110g/4oz diced carrots *(sweet, pungent)*

1 celery stalk, diced *(bitter, astringent)*

3 tablespoons vegetable bouillon powder *(all)*

1 teaspoon ghee *(sweet)*

1 tablespoon mustard seeds *(pungent)*

1 teaspoon ground coriander *(pungent, bitter)*

1 teaspoon turmeric *(bitter, pungent, astringent)*

3cm/1in piece of fresh root ginger, grated, or 1 teaspoon ground ginger *(pungent, sweet)*

1 teaspoon cumin *(pungent)*

2 tablespoons soy sauce *(astringent, salty)*

1. Rinse the lentils well and put in a large saucepan. Add 950ml/1¾ pints of water, the salt, carrots, celery and vegetable bouillon powder to the lentils. Simmer over low heat for about 1 hour, until tender.
2. In a frying pan, heat the ghee to the smoking point. Add the mustard seeds. When they begin to sputter and pop, add to the lentils with the remaining ingredients. Simmer over low heat for about 15 minutes. Serve warm.

Serves 4 to 6

Prominent Tastes: *Pungent, Astringent*	
If you want to reduce	*eat*
VATA	SOME
PITTA	SOME
KAPHA	MORE

♥SPINACH SOUP

◆

The touch of sugar in this recipe softens the bitterness of the spinach – even the children will like it.

25 minutes to prepare

1 tablespoon ghee *(sweet)*

1.6kg/3½ lb spinach, cleaned *(bitter)*

6 celery stalks, cut into bite-sized pieces *(bitter, astringent)*

5 tablespoons vegetable bouillon powder *(all)*

6 tablespoons soy sauce *(astringent, salty)*

1 teaspoon natural (unrefined) sugar *(sweet)*

1 tablespoon tarragon *(pungent)*

1 tablespoon thyme *(pungent)*

½ teaspoon grated nutmeg plus extra, for sprinkling *(pungent, astringent)*

Low-fat plain yoghurt *(sweet, sour)*

1. In a large saucepan, heat the ghee to the smoking point. Sauté the spinach until just tender. Barely cover with water and add everything but the nutmeg and yoghurt. Simmer for about 10 minutes.
2. Add ½ teaspoon nutmeg and blend in a food processor. Serve warm, with a sprinkling of nutmeg and a scoop of yoghurt.

Serves 4 to 6

Prominent Tastes: *Bitter, Astringent, Pungent, Sweet*	
If you want to reduce	*eat*
VATA	LESS
PITTA	MORE
KAPHA	SOME

♥ Watermelon Soup

(WITH BEETROOT AND ORANGE)

◆

This is a low-fat, cooling summer soup.

1 hour to prepare

½ teaspoon ghee *(sweet)*

30g/1oz chopped shallots *(pungent, sweet)*

900g/2 lbs raw beetroot, scrubbed and chopped *(bitter, sweet)*

3 tablespoons vegetable bouillon powder *(all)*

900g/2 lbs watermelon, cut up and seeded *(sweet)*

950ml/1¾ pints orange juice *(sweet, sour)*

Pinch of sea salt *(salty)*

Low-fat plain yoghurt *(sweet, sour)*

Grated nutmeg *(pungent, astringent)*

Fresh mint sprigs *(pungent)*

1. Heat the ghee to the smoking point in a large saucepan. Sauté the shallots until soft. Add the beetroot, vegetable bouillon powder and 950ml/ 1¾ pints of water. Bring to a boil and simmer until the beetroot is thoroughly cooked and tender. Add the watermelon.

2. Blend the soup in the pan with a hand-held soup blender or process in a food processor. Add the orange juice and salt and beat with a large wooden spoon until well mixed.

3. Serve at room temperature in soup bowls with a dollop of yoghurt, a sprinkling of nutmeg and a sprig of fresh mint.

Serves 4 to 6

Prominent Tastes: *Bitter, Sweet*	
If you want to reduce	*eat*
VATA	MORE
PITTA	LESS
KAPHA	MORE

SALADS

◆

Salads can add delightful colour, texture and taste to a meal. Use your imagination when putting salads and dressings together.

CHAPATTI SHELL
SALAD

CLASSIC CHOPPED
SALAD

CURRIED TEMPEH
SALAD

LENTIL-RICE SALAD

SPINACH WITH
GORGONZOLA

THREE FRUIT SALAD

VEGETARIAN NIÇOISE

WARM WILD RICE
SALAD

♥Chapatti Shell Salad

•

45 minutes to prepare

6 Wholemeal Chapattis (page 146) *(sweet)*

400g/14oz cooked chickpeas *(sweet, astringent)*

140g/5oz raw fresh sweetcorn kernels *(sweet)*

140g/5oz fresh or frozen organic peas, thawed *(sweet, astringent)*

30g/1oz chopped spring onions *(pungent, sweet)*

90g/3oz carrots *(sweet, pungent)*

60g/2oz chopped celery *(bitter, astringent)*

30g/1oz chopped fresh coriander *(pungent)*

Juice of 3 limes *(sour)*

1 tablespoon honey or natural (unrefined) sugar *(sweet)*

1 tablespoon soy sauce *(astringent, salty)*

140g/5oz shredded romaine or cos lettuce *(bitter, astringent)*

1. Preheat the oven to 200°C/400°F/gas mark 6.
2. Brush the chapattis on both sides with warm salted water. Place 6 small ovenproof bowls upside down on a baking sheet and drape each chapatti over a bowl. Place in the hot oven and bake for approximately 20 minutes, or until the chapattis are browned. Remove from the oven and cool.
3. Combine the remaining ingredients except the shredded lettuce. Arrange the lettuce in the shells and spoon the salad filling on top.

Serves 6

Prominent Tastes: *Tridoshic*	
If you want to reduce	*eat*
VATA	SOME
PITTA	SOME
KAPHA	SOME

♥Classic Chopped Salad
◆

This salad can be designed for your dosha by using your favourite vegetables and doshic dressing.

30 minutes to prepare

1 broccoli floret *(bitter, astringent)*

1 head of cauliflower *(sweet, astringent)*

450g/1lb asparagus *(sweet, bitter, astringent)*

140g/5oz green beans *(sweet, astringent)*

140g/5oz fresh sweetcorn *(sweet)*

40g/1½oz currants *(sweet)*

30g/1oz pine nuts *(sweet)*

30g/1oz finely chopped red onion *(pungent, sweet)*

1 yellow tomato, chopped and drained *(sweet, sour)*

90g/3oz grated carrots *(sweet, pungent)*

30g/1oz finely chopped fennel *(pungent)*

3 tablespoons **Vata, Pitta,** or **Kapha** dressing of your choice (page 77)

1. Chop the broccoli, cauliflower, asparagus and beans into bite-sized pieces. Lightly steam about 3 minutes. Rinse in cold water and let cool to room temperature.
2. Combine with the remaining ingredients and toss with the dressing.

Serves 4 to 6

Prominent Tastes: *Tridoshic*	
If you want to reduce	*eat*
VATA	SOME
PITTA	SOME
KAPHA	MORE

♥Curried Tempeh Salad
•

This tastes so much like chicken, you'll fool those meat eaters.

45 minutes to prepare

2 × 230g/8oz packages soy tempeh *(sweet, astringent)*

3 tablespoons minced fresh coriander *(pungent)*

3 tablespoons chopped fresh parsley *(pungent, astringent)*

30g/1oz chopped almonds *(sweet, bitter)*

40g/1½ oz raisins/currants *(sweet)*

30g/1oz chopped celery *(bitter, astringent)*

1 teaspoon turmeric *(bitter, pungent, astringent)*

1 teaspoon garam masala of coriander, cumin, cardamom and cinnamon *(pungent, bitter, sweet)*

1 tablespoon soy sauce *(astringent, salty)*

60g/2oz low-fat plain yoghurt *(sweet, sour)*

Pinch of sea salt *(salty)*

Shredded romaine or cos lettuce *(bitter, astringent)*

Fresh parsley or coriander sprigs *(pungent, astringent)*

1. Steam the tempeh in the top of a double boiler for 20 minutes. Cool and crumble with your fingers. Combine all the ingredients except lettuce and parsley or coriander in a large bowl and toss well.
2. Make into rounds. Serve on a bed of lettuce and garnish with parsley or coriander sprigs.

Serves 4 to 6

Prominent Tastes: *Sweet, Astringent, Bitter, Pungent*	
If you want to reduce	*eat*
VATA	MORE
PITTA	MORE
KAPHA	LESS

♥Lentil-Rice Salad
♦

Lentils and rice together create complete protein.
Serve this dish on a warm day with Tomato Chutney (page 172)
and Wholemeal Chapattis (page 146).

25 minutes to prepare

3 carrots, chopped *(sweet, pungent)*
450g/1lb cooked brown or green
   lentils, cooled *(sweet, astringent)*
140g/5oz cooked basmati rice,
   cooled *(sweet)*
110g/4oz chopped celery *(bitter,*
   astringent)
140g/5oz cooked fresh or frozen
   organic peas, cooled *(sweet,*
   astringent)

2 tablespoons finely chopped spring
   onions *(pungent, sweet)*
2 tablespoons chopped fresh parsley
   (pungent, astringent)
3 tablespoons **Vata, Pitta,** or
   Kapha dressing of your choice
   (page 77)

1. Blanch the carrots by immersing in a pan of boiling water for 5 minutes.
   Remove from the pan and immediately rinse until cooled with cold
   water to stop the cooking and retain colour.
2. Combine all the ingredients in a bowl and gently toss with the dressing.

Serves 4 to 6

Prominent Tastes: *Tridoshic*	
If you want to reduce	*eat*
VATA	SOME
PITTA	MORE
KAPHA	MORE

Spinach with Gorgonzola

◆

This is a quick, delicious salad.

20 minutes to prepare

900g/2 lbs washed and stemmed
spinach *(bitter)*
1 cup Honey-Glazed Walnuts,
recipe follows *(sweet)*
110g/4oz crumbled Gorgonzola
cheese *(sweet)*

90g/3oz currants *(sweet)*
3 tablespoons Poppy Seed Dressing
(page 80)

Toss all ingredients together and arrange on plates.

HONEY-GLAZED WALNUTS

½ teaspoon ghee *(sweet)*
90g/3oz walnut pieces *(sweet)*

1 tablespoon honey *(sweet)*

1. Heat the ghee to the smoking point in a frying pan. Toss in the walnuts
   and sauté 2 minutes, until golden.
2. Add the honey and coat the walnuts well. Let cool completely before
   using.

Serves 4 to 6

Prominent Tastes: *Bitter, Sweet*	
If you want to reduce	eat
VATA	MORE
PITTA	MORE
KAPHA	SOME

Three Fruit Salad

◆

Tomatoes a fruit? Yes. Avocados a fruit? Yes. This salad is more like a chutney and goes well with spicy main dishes. If you can't find yellow tomatoes, red ones will do just as well. Make this in summer, though, when tomatoes are vine ripened and flavourful.

10 minutes to prepare

1 large firm but ripe yellow tomato, diced and drained *(sweet, sour)*

1 firm avocado, diced *(sweet)*

2 firm but ripe nectarines, diced (do not remove skin) *(sweet)*

⅛ teaspoon balsamic vinegar *(sour)*

1 teaspoon dried minced onion *(pungent, sweet)*

1 teaspoon honey, optional *(sweet)*

1 teaspoon olive oil *(sweet)*

1 teaspoon orange juice *(sweet, sour)*

1 tablespoon soy sauce *(astringent, salty)*

4 to 6 romaine or cos lettuce leaves *(bitter, astringent)*

Combine all the ingredients except lettuce in a bowl and toss gently. Serve on lettuce leaves.

Serves 4 to 6

Prominent Tastes: *Sweet, Pungent*	
If you want to reduce	*eat*
VATA	MORE
PITTA	LESS
KAPHA	LESS

Vegetarian Niçoise

◆

*Although tuna is traditionally included in this salad,
you'll never miss it.*

30 minutes to prepare

2 heads of romaine or cos lettuce,
washed, dried and shredded
(bitter, astringent)

6 plum tomatoes, cut into bite-sized
pieces and drained *(sweet, sour)*

½ sweet red onion, finely chopped
(pungent, sweet)

1 cucumber, peeled, seeded and
chopped *(sweet, astringent)*

1 small jicama, peeled and chopped
(optional) *(sweet)*

2 tablespoons finely chopped fresh
parsley *(pungent)*

175g/6oz capers, drained, juice
reserved *(astringent, salty)*

60–90g/2–3oz crumbled feta cheese
(sweet)

30ml/1 fl oz olive oil *(sweet)*

30ml/1 fl oz orange juice *(sweet,
sour)*

1 tablespoon soy sauce *(astringent,
salty)*

1 teaspoon balsamic vinegar *(sour)*

1 teaspoon honey (optional) *(sweet)*

1. Arrange the lettuce on a large platter. Carefully layer the tomatoes,
   onion, cucumber, jicama, if using, parsley and capers in an attractive
   pattern over the lettuce.
2. Combine the remaining ingredients, including the reserved caper juice,
   in a jar, shake well, and pour over the salad.

Serves 4 to 8

Prominent Tastes: *Sweet, Astringent, Sour*	
If you want to reduce	*eat*
VATA	SOME
PITTA	SOME
KAPHA	SOME

Warm Wild Rice Salad

◆

In this different combination the sweetness is balanced by the fennel and fresh herbs.

45 minutes to prepare

450g/16oz cooked mixed wild and brown rice, cooled *(sweet)*

2 avocados, cut into bite-sized pieces *(sweet)*

80g/2½oz diced fresh fennel bulb or 2 tablespoons fennel seeds *(pungent)*

110g/4oz diced celery *(bitter, astringent)*

140g/4½oz dried cranberries *(sweet, astringent)*

30g/1oz sunflower seeds *(sweet, bitter)*

40g/1½oz raisins *(sweet)*

2 tablespoons chopped fresh dill *(pungent)*

2 tablespoons chopped fresh chives *(pungent)*

Lemon-Lime Dressing, to taste (page 84)

Combine all the ingredients in a bowl and serve at room temperature.

Serves 6 to 8

Prominent Tastes: *Sweet, Pungent*	
If you want to reduce	*eat*
VATA	MORE
PITTA	MORE
KAPHA	LESS

RAITAS

◆

Raitas are salads made with yoghurt. They are traditionally served as cooling side dishes to accompany spicy meals.

CHICKPEA RAITA	PEAR-DATE RAITA
CUCUMBER RAITA	POTATO RAITA

♥Chickpea Raita

◆

25 minutes to prepare

1 teaspoon mustard oil or ghee *(pungent or sweet)*

1 teaspoon black mustard seeds *(pungent)*

1 teaspoon cumin seeds *(pungent)*

400g/14oz cooked chickpeas *(sweet, astringent)*

1 large cucumber, cut into bite-sized pieces *(sweet, astringent)*

40g/1½oz currants *(sweet)*

1 teaspoon crushed chillies *(pungent)*

3 tablespoons finely chopped spring onions *(pungent, sweet)*

1 tablespoon finely chopped fresh coriander *(pungent)*

2 tablespoons soy sauce *(astringent, salty)*

230g/8oz low-fat plain yoghurt *(sweet, sour)*

Juice of 1 lemon *(sour, astringent)*

1. Heat the oil or ghee in a small frying pan. Toss in the mustard and cumin seeds. When they sputter and pop, remove from the heat. Cool completely.

2. Toss gently with the remaining ingredients. Refrigerate until 1 hour before serving.

Serves 4 to 6

Prominent Tastes: *Pungent, Sweet, Sour*	
If you want to reduce	eat
VATA	SOME
PITTA	LESS
KAPHA	LESS

♥Cucumber Raita

◆

25 minutes to prepare

2 medium cucumbers, peeled, seeded and diced *(sweet, astringent)*

110g/4oz low-fat plain yoghurt *(sweet, sour)*

1 tablespoon minced spring onions *(pungent, sweet)*

3cm/1in piece of fresh root ginger, grated, or ½ teaspoon ground ginger *(pungent, sweet)*

2 tablespoons finely chopped fresh coriander *(pungent)*

Juice of 1 lemon *(sour, astringent)*

1 teaspoon honey *(sweet)*

⅛ teaspoon lemon zest *(bitter)*

⅛ teaspoon turmeric *(bitter, pungent, astringent)*

⅛ teaspoon cinnamon *(pungent, bitter)*

⅛ teaspoon cardamom *(pungent, sweet)*

2 tablespoons soy sauce *(astringent, salty)*

Combine all the ingredients in a mixing bowl and toss gently. Refrigerate until 1 hour before serving.

Serves 4 to 6

Prominent Tastes: *Tridoshic*	
If you want to reduce	*eat*
VATA	SOME
PITTA	SOME
KAPHA	SOME

$\mathcal{P}$ear-$\mathcal{D}$ate $\mathcal{R}$aita

◆

Replace the pears with apples for a Waldorf salad.

20 minutes to prepare

10 Anjou or Williams pears, chopped *(sweet)*

170g/6oz chopped dates *(sweet)*

90g/3oz raisins *(sweet)*

60g/2oz chopped celery *(bitter, astringent)*

60g/2oz toasted pine nuts *(sweet)*

Juice of 2 lemons *(sour, astringent)*

110g/4oz low-fat plain yoghurt *(sweet, sour)*

60ml/2 fl oz honey *(sweet)*

Toss all the ingredients together in a bowl. Refrigerate until 1 hour before serving.

Serves 6 to 8

Prominent Tastes: *Astringent, Sweet*	
If you want to reduce	*eat*
VATA	MORE
PITTA	SOME
KAPHA	LESS

♥Potato Raita

•

40 minutes to prepare

1 teaspoon mustard oil or ghee
   (pungent or sweet)

1 teaspoon black mustard seeds
   (pungent)

1 teaspoon cumin seeds *(pungent)*

3 medium potatoes, preferably
   yellow or red, scrubbed and cut
   into bite-sized pieces *(astringent)*

1 teaspoon crushed chillies *(pungent)*

3 tablespoons finely chopped spring
   onions *(pungent, sweet)*

1 tablespoon finely chopped fresh
   coriander *(pungent)*

2 tablespoons soy sauce *(astringent,
   salty)*

230g/8oz low-fat plain yoghurt
   (sweet, sour)

Juice of 1 lemon *(sour, astringent)*

1. Heat the oil or ghee in a small frying pan. Toss in the mustard and
   cumin seeds. When they sputter and pop, add the potatoes and crushed
   chillies. Sauté, stirring frequently, until the potatoes are cooked, approximately 20 minutes. Cool completely.

2. Toss gently with the remaining ingredients. Refrigerate until 1 hour
   before serving.

Serves 4 to 6

Prominent Tastes: *Astringent, Pungent, Sour*	
If you want to reduce	*eat*
VATA	MORE
PITTA	LESS
KAPHA	SOME

Salad Dressings

◆

Our salad dressings are mostly low- or non-fat, providing a variety of tastes. Be sure to keep the oils and other ingredients for each dosha on hand, since many of the dressings are dosha specific.

BASIC CREAMY TOFU
DRESSING

BASIC MISO DRESSING

POPPY SEED DRESSING

MINTED CITRUS
DRESSING

MUSTARD DRESSING

YOGHURT DILL DRESSING

LEMON-LIME
DRESSING

♥ BASIC CREAMY TOFU DRESSING
•

Add herbs and spices to create individual flavours.

15 minutes to prepare

For Vata

5cm/2in piece of firm tofu *(sweet, astringent)*

1 tablespoon honey *(sweet)*

1 tablespoon soy sauce *(astringent, salty)*

1 tablespoon lemon juice *(sweet, sour)*

110ml/4 fl oz orange juice *(sweet, sour)*

For Pitta

5cm/2in piece of firm tofu *(sweet, astringent)*

1 tablespoon natural (unrefined) sugar *(sweet)*

1 tablespoon soy sauce *(astringent, salty)*

1 tablespoon unfiltered apple juice *(sour)*

110ml/4 fl oz orange juice *(sweet, astringent)*

For Kapha

2.5cm/1in piece of firm tofu *(sweet, astringent)*

1 tablespoon honey *(sweet)*

1 tablespoon soy sauce *(astringent, salty)*

1 tablespoon lemon juice *(sweet, sour)*

110ml/4 fl oz unfiltered apple juice *(sweet, astringent)*

Place the ingredients in a liquidizer or food processor and blend. The dressing can be stored in the refrigerator for several days.

Makes about 170ml/6 fl oz

Prominent Tastes: *Sweet, Sour*	
If you want to reduce	eat
VATA	SOME
PITTA	SOME
KAPHA	SOME

❤ Basic Miso Dressing

◆

This is a dressing for all seasons, for all doshas.

15 minutes to prepare

For Vata

1 tablespoon white miso paste *(astringent)*

1 tablespoon honey *(sweet)*

1 tablespoon soy sauce *(astringent, salty)*

1 tablespoon lemon juice *(sweet, sour)*

110ml/4 fl oz orange juice *(sweet, sour)*

For Pitta

2 tablespoons white miso paste *(astringent)*

1 tablespoon natural (unrefined) sugar *(sweet)*

1 tablespoon soy sauce *(astringent, salty)*

1 tablespoon unfiltered apple juice *(sweet, sour)*

110ml/4 fl oz orange juice *(sweet, sour)*

For Kapha

2 tablespoons white miso paste *(astringent)*

1 tablespoon honey *(sweet)*

1 tablespoon soy sauce *(astringent, salty)*

1 tablespoon lemon juice *(sweet, sour)*

110ml/4 fl oz unfiltered apple juice *(sweet, sour)*

Place the ingredients in a liquidizer or food processor and blend. The dressing can be stored in the refrigerator for several days.

Makes about 170ml/6 fl oz

Prominent Tastes: *Sweet, Astringent, Sour*	
If you want to reduce	*eat*
VATA	SOME
PITTA	SOME
KAPHA	SOME

♥Poppy Seed Dressing

◆

Try Poppy Seed Dressing on a melon or other fruit.

15 minutes to prepare

For Vata

1 tablespoon Dijon mustard *(pungent)*

1 tablespoon olive oil *(sweet)*

1 tablespoon honey *(sweet)*

1 tablespoon soy sauce *(astringent, salty)*

1 tablespoon lemon juice *(sweet, sour)*

110ml/4 fl oz orange juice *(sweet, sour)*

60g/2oz low-fat plain yoghurt *(sweet, sour)*

1 tablespoon poppy seeds *(pungent, astringent, sweet)*

For Pitta

1 tablespoon Dijon mustard *(pungent)*

1 tablespoon olive oil *(sweet)*

1 tablespoon natural (unrefined) sugar *(sweet)*

1 tablespoon soy sauce *(astringent, salty)*

1 tablespoon unfiltered apple juice *(sweet, sour)*

110ml/4 fl oz orange juice *(sweet, sour)*

60g/2oz low-fat plain yoghurt *(sweet, sour)*

1 tablespoon poppy seeds *(pungent, astringent, sweet)*

For Kapha

1 tablespoon Dijon mustard *(pungent)*

1 tablespoon almond oil *(sweet)*

1 tablespoon honey *(sweet)*

1 tablespoon soy sauce *(astringent, salty)*

1 tablespoon lemon juice *(sweet, sour)*

110ml/4 fl oz unfiltered apple juice *(sweet, sour)*

60g/2oz low-fat plain yoghurt *(sweet, sour)*

1 tablespoon poppy seeds *(pungent, astringent, sweet)*

Combine all the ingredients in a small jar and shake well. The dressing can be stored in the refrigerator for several days.

Makes about 170ml/6 fl oz

Prominent Tastes: *Pungent, Sweet, Sour*	
If you want to reduce	*eat*
VATA	SOME
PITTA	SOME
KAPHA	SOME

ℳɪɴᴛᴇᴅ ℭɪᴛʀᴜs 𝒟ʀᴇssɪɴɢ

◆

This is a tangy, cooling dressing.

15 minutes to prepare

Juice of 4 lemons *(sour, astringent)*

Juice of 2 oranges *(sweet, sour)*

2 tablespoons honey, or natural (unrefined) sugar *(sweet)*

3 tablespoons soy sauce *(astringent, salty)*

1 tablespoon olive oil *(sweet)*

2 tablespoons crushed dried mint or 1 tablespoon minced fresh mint *(pungent)*

Place all the ingredients in a jar and shake. The dressing can be stored in the refrigerator for several days.

Makes about 230ml/8 fl oz

Prominent Tastes: *Sweet, Sour*	
If you want to reduce	*eat*
VATA	MORE
PITTA	SOME
KAPHA	LESS

♥Mustard Dressing

◆

This dressing is great on salads, potatoes or cooked vegetables.

15 minutes to prepare

For Vata

2 tablespoons Dijon mustard *(pungent)*

1 tablespoon olive oil *(sweet)*

1 tablespoon honey *(sweet)*

1 tablespoon soy sauce *(astringent, salty)*

1 tablespoon lemon juice *(sweet, sour)*

110ml/4 fl oz orange juice *(sweet, sour)*

For Pitta

2 tablespoons Dijon mustard *(pungent)*

1 tablespoon olive oil *(sweet)*

1 tablespoon natural (unrefined) sugar *(sweet)*

1 tablespoon soy sauce *(astringent, salty)*

1 tablespoon apple juice *(sweet, sour)*

110ml/4 fl oz orange juice *(sweet, sour)*

For Kapha

2 tablespoons Dijon mustard *(pungent)*

1 tablespoon almond oil *(sweet)*

1 tablespoon honey *(sweet)*

1 tablespoon soy sauce *(astringent, salty)*

1 tablespoon lemon juice *(sweet, sour)*

110ml/4 fl oz unfiltered apple juice *(sweet, sour)*

Combine all ingredients in a jar and shake well. The dressing can be stored in the refrigerator for several days.

Makes about 170ml/6 fl oz

Prominent Tastes: *Pungent, Sweet, Sour*	
If you want to reduce	*eat*
VATA	SOME
PITTA	SOME
KAPHA	SOME

♥ Yoghurt Dill Dressing
◆

15 minutes to prepare

For Vata

1 tablespoon olive oil *(sweet)*

1 tablespoon honey *(sweet)*

1 tablespoon soy sauce *(astringent, salty)*

1 tablespoon lemon juice *(sweet, sour)*

110ml/4 fl oz orange juice *(sweet, sour)*

60g/2oz low-fat plain yoghurt *(sweet, sour)*

2 tablespoons minced fresh dill *(pungent)*

For Pitta

1 tablespoon olive oil *(sweet)*

1 tablespoon natural (unrefined) sugar *(sweet)*

1 tablespoon soy sauce *(astringent, salty)*

1 tablespoon unfiltered apple juice *(sweet, sour)*

110ml/4 fl oz orange juice *(sweet, sour)*

60g/2oz low-fat plain yoghurt *(sweet, sour)*

2 tablespoons minced fresh dill *(pungent)*

For Kapha

1 tablespoon sunflower oil *(sweet)*

1 tablespoon honey *(sweet)*

1 tablespoon soy sauce *(astringent, salty)*

1 tablespoon lemon juice *(sweet, sour)*

110ml/4 fl oz unfiltered apple juice *(sweet, sour)*

60g/2oz low-fat plain yoghurt *(sweet, sour)*

2 tablespoons minced fresh dill *(pungent)*

Combine all the ingredients in a small jar and shake well. The dressing can be stored in the refrigerator for several days.

Makes about 170 ml/6 fl oz

Prominent Tastes: *Sweet, Sour, Astringent*	
If you want to reduce	*eat*
VATA	SOME
PITTA	SOME
KAPHA	SOME

Lemon-Lime Dressing

◆

15 minutes to prepare

For Vata

1 tablespoon olive oil *(sweet)*

1 tablespoon honey *(sweet)*

1 tablespoon soy sauce *(astringent, salty)*

1 tablespoon lemon juice *(sweet, sour)*

110ml/4 fl oz lime juice *(sweet, sour)*

For Pitta

1 tablespoon olive oil

1 tablespoon natural (unrefined) sugar

1 tablespoon soy sauce *(astringent, salty)*

1 tablespoon lemon juice *(sweet, sour)*

110ml/4 fl oz lime juice *(sweet, sour)*

For Kapha

1 tablespoon sunflower oil *(sweet)*

1 tablespoon honey *(sweet)*

1 tablespoon soy sauce *(astringent, salty)*

1 tablespoon lemon juice *(sweet, sour)*

110ml/4 fl oz lime juice *(sweet, sour)*

Combine all the ingredients in a small jar and shake well. The dressing can be stored in the refrigerator for several days.

Makes about 230ml/8 fl oz

Prominent Tastes: *Sweet, Sour*	
If you want to reduce	*eat*
VATA	SOME
PITTA	SOME
KAPHA	SOME

Main Dishes

◆

Our main dishes offer variety without restricting you to Indian food, although we use many Ayurvedic spices and herbs. Combined with certain side dishes, salads and breads (see chapter 7, Menu Planning), these dishes help provide nutritional balance. Pass the *churans* to your family and friends for further doshic satisfaction.

Most of these dishes are easy to prepare. Preparation time is approximate, allowing for individual variation.

PASTA WITH MADEIRA
MUSHROOM SAUCE

CARROT CROQUETTES
WITH REDCURRANT
SAUCE

SPINACH PESTO

CHEESELESS LASAGNE

MUSHROOM
STROGANOFF

PIZZA

SPINACH PIZZA
RUSTICA

POTATO-LEEK FRITTATA

VEGETABLE BARLEY
CASSEROLE

TOFU SATAY

VEGETABLE CHOW MEIN

VEGETABLE TOFU
CRUSTLESS PIE

VEGETABLE PANEER
TART

VEGETABLE STRUDEL

BAKED WINTER SQUASH
WITH WILD RICE-
CRANBERRY STUFFING

VEGGIE BURGERS

COSMIC CURRY

COSMIC CURRY
ENCHILADAS

♥Pasta with Madeira Mushroom Sauce

◆

Light and fast, this is great for surprise guests.
Don't worry, the alcohol burns off.

20 minutes to prepare

1 teaspoon olive oil *(sweet)*

1 large flat mushroom, sliced *(sweet, astringent)*

10 shiitake mushrooms, sliced *(sweet, astringent)*

20 cup mushrooms, sliced *(sweet, astringent)*

1 garlic clove, minced *(all but sour)*

2 tablespoons minced spring onions *(pungent, sweet)*

2 tablespoons chopped fresh parsley *(pungent, astringent)*

Sea salt *(salty)* and pepper *(pungent)*

60ml/2 fl oz Madeira wine *(sweet)*

2 cups cooked pasta of your choice *(sweet)*

1. In a frying pan, heat the oil to the smoking point. Sauté the mushrooms, garlic and spring onions for 2 minutes, stirring frequently.
2. When browned, add the parsley and salt and pepper to taste. Add the Madeira and cook for 2 minutes.
3. Toss with the cooked pasta.

Serves 2 to 4

Prominent Tastes: *Sweet, Astringent*	
If you want to reduce	eat
VATA	MORE
PITTA	SOME
KAPHA	LESS

CARROT CROQUETTES WITH REDCURRANT SAUCE

◆

These are lovely with spinach on the side. **Pittas,** *don't overeat!*

30 minutes to prepare

170g/6oz shredded carrots *(sweet, pungent)*

60g/2oz minced celery *(bitter, astringent)*

310g/11oz cooked rice *(sweet)*

30g/1oz bread crumbs plus extra for rolling *(sweet)*

2 eggs *(sweet)*

90g/3oz raisins *(sweet)*

4 tablespoons soy sauce *(astringent, salty)*

1 tablespoon vegetable seasoning powder *(all)*

Redcurrant Sauce (recipe follows)

1. Preheat the oven to 180°C/350°F/gas mark 4.
2. Combine all the ingredients except the extra bread crumbs and the Redcurrant Sauce in a mixing bowl. Shape into croquettes or patties and roll in the bread crumbs.
3. Bake for about 30 minutes. Serve with the Redcurrant Sauce.

REDCURRANT SAUCE

350g/12oz redcurrant jelly *(sweet)*

2 tablespoons cornflour dissolved in 450ml/16 fl oz orange juice

(sweet, sour)

110g/4oz redcurrants *(sweet)*

Combine all the ingredients in a saucepan. Bring to a boil to thicken. Serve the warm sauce over the croquettes.

Serves 4 to 6

Prominent Taste: *Sweet*	
If you want to reduce	*eat*
VATA	MORE
PITTA	MORE
KAPHA	LESS

Spinach Pesto

◆

*Made without cheese or added oil, this is a
yummy version of an old classic.*

20 minutes to prepare

280g/10oz fresh spinach *(bitter)*

2 avocados, cut into pieces *(sweet)*

110g/4oz fresh coriander *(pungent)*

110g/4oz fresh parsley *(pungent,
astringent)*

110g/4oz fresh basil *(pungent)*

Juice of 1 lemon *(sour, astringent)*

60g/2oz pine nuts *(sweet)*

Sea salt *(salty)*

Pepper *(pungent)*

450g/1 lb pasta of your choice,
cooked and drained *(sweet)*

Combine all the ingredients except the pasta in a food processor and blend
well. Add some water to aid in mixing, if needed. Toss with warm pasta.

Serves 4 to 6

Prominent Tastes: *All*	
If you want to reduce	*eat*
VATA	SOME
PITTA	SOME
KAPHA	SOME

❤Cheeseless Lasagne

◆

This is a hearty, cheeseless version of an old favourite. Sun-dried tomatoes replace tomato sauce for a less sour flavour.

1 hour to prepare

Sauce

1 teaspoon ghee *(sweet)*

6 carrots, cut into 3cm/1in pieces *(sweet, pungent)*

6 courgettes, cut into 3cm/1in pieces *(sweet)*

6 celery stalks, cut into 3cm/1in pieces *(bitter, astringent)*

60g/2oz parsley *(pungent, astringent)*

450g/1 lb sun-dried tomatoes, drained *(sweet, sour)*

1 tablespoon oregano *(pungent)*

Dash of sea salt *(salty)*

2 pinches Italian Seasoning *(pungent)*

Filling

450g/1 lb firm tofu, crumbled *(sweet, astringent)*

230–340ml/8–12 fl oz sauce (from step 1)

60g/2oz ground pine nuts *(sweet)*

450g/16oz lasagne verde, cooked and drained *(bitter, sweet)*

Bread crumbs *(sweet)*

1. In a large frying pan, heat the ghee to the smoking point. Sauté the carrots, courgettes and celery in the ghee for 5 minutes. Combine with the parsley, tomatoes, oregano, salt and Italian Seasoning and grind coarsely in a food processor. Return to the pot and simmer for 5 minutes. Remove from heat and set aside while you prepare the filling.
2. Preheat the oven to 180°C/350°F/gas mark 4.
3. Combine the tofu, sauce and nuts.
4. Layer in the casserole dish as follows: sauce, lasagne, filling, sauce, lasagne, filling, sauce, lasagne, sauce, bread crumbs.
5. Bake, uncovered, for 40 minutes, or until the bread crumbs are golden and the lasagne is bubbling.

Serves 8 to 10

Prominent Tastes: *Sweet, Astringent, Pungent*	
If you want to reduce	*eat*
VATA	MORE
PITTA	SOME
KAPHA	SOME

❤ᗰushroom Stroganoff

◆

Beef Stroganoff was never this good.

25 minutes to prepare

1 large flat mushroom *(sweet, astringent)*

10 shiitake mushrooms *(sweet, astringent)*

450g/1 lb mushrooms *(sweet, astringent)*

1 teaspoon olive oil *(sweet)*

1 garlic clove, minced *(all but sour)*

½ yellow onion, chopped *(pungent, sweet)*

1 tablespoon soy sauce *(astringent, salty)*

1 tablespoon vegetable bouillon powder *(all)*

1 tablespoon cornflour mixed with 110ml/4 fl oz water *(sweet)*

110g/4oz low-fat plain yoghurt *(sweet, sour)*

1 teaspoon tarragon *(pungent)*

2 tablespoons chopped fresh parsley *(pungent, astringent)*

Dash of grated nutmeg *(pungent)*

310g/11oz cooked basmati rice or 230g/8oz pasta of your choice, cooked and drained *(sweet)*

Fresh parsley sprigs *(pungent, astringent)*

1. Cut all the mushrooms into bite-sized pieces, using most of the stems.
2. In a large frying pan, heat the oil to the smoking point. Add the mushrooms, garlic and onion. Sauté for 5 minutes, until the mushrooms are browned.

3. Add the remaining ingredients except the rice or pasta and parsley sprigs and simmer for 1 minute, until thickened.

4. Serve over rice or pasta and garnish with the parsley sprigs.

Serves 4 to 6

Prominent Tastes: *Sweet, Pungent, Astringent*	
If you want to reduce	*eat*
VATA	MORE
PITTA	SOME
KAPHA	LESS

♥𝒫IZZA

◆

Be creative with this: provide a variety of vegetables and allow each person to build the perfect personal pizza for his or her body type.

1½ hours to prepare

Pizza Dough

230ml/8 fl oz warm water

1 sachet (7g/¼ oz) fast acting dried yeast

1 tablespoon natural (unrefined) sugar *(sweet)*

300–340g/10–12oz organic unbleached strong white flour or 230g/8oz white and 110g/4oz organic wholemeal flour *(sweet, astringent)*

2 tablespoons olive oil *(sweet)*

½ teaspoon sea salt *(salty)*

1. Combine the water, yeast, sugar and half the flour in a large bowl. Mix well. Add the oil and salt. Gradually add the rest of the flour. Mix with a large wooden spoon until a soft dough is achieved.

2. Place the dough on a lightly floured surface and knead 5 minutes. If the dough is too sticky, sprinkle with extra flour. Place the dough in a lightly oiled bowl and let rise until doubled, about 45 minutes.

3. After the dough has risen, place on a lightly floured surface and divide into 2 equal parts. Cover with a towel and let stand for 20 minutes. Shape into 4 mini pizzas or 1 large pizza.

4. Preheat the oven to 200°C/400°F/gas mark 6.

5. Top the pizza with:
   Organic Pizza Sauce
   Oregano or Italian Seasonings
   Shredded vegetables of your choice
   Grated Parmesan cheese (optional)

6. Bake for 20 minutes, or until the crust is golden.

Makes 4 23cm/10in pizzas or 1 40cm/16in pizza

Prominent Taste: *Sweet*	
If you want to reduce	*eat*
VATA	MORE
PITTA	SOME
KAPHA	SOME

Spinach Pizza Rustica

◆

This is a filling main dish for a special luncheon.
Serve with a green salad.

2 hours to prepare

2 teaspoons ghee or olive oil *(sweet)*

2 large leeks, chopped and well
  washed *(pungent, sweet)*

900g/2 lbs spinach, washed and
  chopped *(bitter)*

5 medium yellow potatoes,
  chopped *(astringent)*

2 eggs, beaten *(sweet)*

1 teaspoon sea salt *(salty)*

¼ teaspoon tarragon *(pungent)*

60g/2oz chopped walnuts or
  pine nuts *(sweet)*

Pizza Rustica Dough

450g/1 lb organic unbleached strong
  white flour or organic wholemeal
  flour *(sweet, astringent)*

1 teaspoon natural (unrefined)
  sugar *(sweet)*

1 teaspoon sea salt *(salty)*

110g/4oz cold butter, cut into bits
  (sweet)

4 large eggs, beaten *(sweet)*

Egg glaze made from 1 egg beaten
  with 2 tablespoons water *(sweet)*

Bread crumbs *(sweet)*

1. In a large frying pan, heat 1 teaspoon ghee or oil to the smoking point.
   Sauté the leeks until browned. Add the spinach and continue cooking
   until the spinach is wilted. Place in a bowl.

2. Heat the frying pan again, add the remaining 1 teaspoon ghee or oil,
   and sauté the potatoes until browned, about 15 minutes. Place in the
   bowl with the spinach and leeks. Toss with the eggs, salt, tarragon and
   walnuts or pine nuts. Cool.

3. Preheat the oven to 190°C/375°F/gas mark 5.

4. Make the Pizza Rustica Dough: Place the dry ingredients in a food
   processor and blend. Add the butter and pulse the machine until the
   mixture resembles coarse meal. Add the eggs and pulse until the eggs are
   incorporated and the dough is formed. Don't overprocess. Wrap the

dough in clingfilm and chill for 1 hour.

5. Roll the dough into a large circle on a floured surface. Place in a large cake tin, pizza pan or pie tin and spoon in the filling. Fold over the edges of dough and brush with the egg glaze. Sprinkle with the bread crumbs.

6. Bake for about 1 hour, or until the crust is golden brown. (The dough can be made ahead and chilled in the pan, covered.) Serve warm or at room temperature.

Serves 6 to 8

Prominent Tastes: *Sweet, Astringent, Bitter*	
If you want to reduce	*eat*
VATA	SOME
PITTA	SOME
KAPHA	SOME

$\mathcal{P}$OTATO-$\mathcal{L}$EEK $\mathcal{F}$RITTATA

◆

*Yellow-flesh potatoes add a special quality to this dish, but
ordinary white potatoes may also be used.*

1½ hours to prepare

1 teaspoon ghee *(sweet)*

1 large leek, diced and washed
thoroughly *(pungent, sweet)*

450g/1 lb yellow potatoes, diced
(astringent)

4 eggs, beaten *(sweet)*

2 tablespoons vegetable bouillon
powder *(all)*

1 tablespoon soy sauce *(astringent,
salty)*

½ teaspoon thyme *(pungent)*

½ teaspoon tarragon *(pungent)*

130g/4½oz ground pine nuts
(sweet)

1. Preheat the oven to 180°C/350°F/gas mark 4.
2. In a frying pan, heat ½ teaspoon ghee to the smoking point. Add the leek
   and cook until softened, about 5 minutes. Remove and place in a bowl.
3. Heat the remaining ½ teaspoon ghee in the frying pan to the smoking
   point. Add the potatoes and cook, stirring frequently, until browned
   and cooked but still firm. Combine with the remaining ingredients
   except 2 tablespoons pine nuts.
4. Pour into a lightly oiled 23 × 30cm/9 × 12in baking dish and top with
   the remaining pine nuts. Bake, uncovered, for 30 to 40 minutes. Serve
   warm.

Serves 6 to 8

Prominent Tastes: *Sweet, Pungent, Astringent*	
If you want to reduce	*eat*
VATA	SOME
PITTA	SOME
KAPHA	SOME

♥ Vegetable Barley Casserole

◆

1½ hours to prepare

450g/1 lb bite-sized vegetables, such as carrots *(sweet, pungent)*, courgettes *(sweet)*, yellow squash *(sweet)*, potatoes *(astringent)* and leeks *(pungent, sweet)*

1 tablespoon ghee *(sweet)*

450g/1 lb cooked barley *(sweet)*

140g/5oz fresh or frozen corn (if using frozen corn, choose organic if possible and thaw) *(sweet)*

140g/5oz fresh or frozen peas (if using frozen peas, choose organic if possible and thaw) *(sweet, astringent)*

2 tablespoons thyme *(pungent)*

1 tablespoon oregano *(pungent)*

4 tablespoons soy sauce *(astringent, salty)*

3 tablespoons vegetable bouillon powder *(all)*

230ml/8 fl oz organic tomato sauce *(sweet, sour)*

2 tablespoons arrowroot dissolved in 110ml/4 fl oz water

Bread crumbs, for topping *(sweet)*

1. Preheat the oven to 180°C/350°F/gas mark 4.
2. In a large frying pan, sauté the bite-sized vegetables in the ghee. Combine with the rest of the ingredients except the bread crumbs.
3. Pour into an oiled 23 × 30cm/9 × 12 in casserole dish and sprinkle liberally with the bread crumbs. Bake for about 40 minutes, or until bubbling.

Serves 8 to 10

Prominent Tastes: *Sweet, Astringent*	
If you want to reduce	*eat*
VATA	SOME
PITTA	MORE
KAPHA	MORE

Tofu Satay

◆

*Who needs chicken? This warm, spicy dish is so good,
you'll be back for more.*

1 hour to prepare

1 piece of very firm tofu *(sweet, astringent)*

2 tablespoons vegetable bouillon powder *(all)*

1 tablespoon soy sauce *(astringent, salty)*

2.5cm/1in piece of fresh root ginger, peeled and crushed *(pungent, sweet)*

1 tablespoon sesame oil *(sweet)*

Satay Sauce

1 garlic clove, optional *(all but sour)*

60g/2oz peanut butter *(sweet, astringent)*

110ml/4 fl oz orange juice *(sweet, sour)*

400ml/14 fl oz coconut milk *(sweet)*

1 teaspoon Thai-style chilli paste *(pungent)*

2 tablespoons dried minced onion *(pungent, sweet)*

3 tablespoons soy sauce *(astringent, salty)*

60ml/2 fl oz satay sauce *(pungent)*

2 tablespoons chopped fresh coriander *(pungent)*

450g/1 lb cooked basmati rice *(sweet)*

Fresh coriander sprigs *(pungent)* and thin lemon slices *(sour, astringent)*, for garnish

1. Press the tofu between layers of kitchen paper. Place one plate on each side of the paper and press down to express as much liquid from the tofu as possible. Cut the tofu into 2.5cm/1in cubes.

2. Bring 700ml/1¼ pints of water, the vegetable bouillon powder, the tablespoon of soy sauce and ginger to a boil. Immerse the tofu cubes in this broth and simmer 15 minutes. Drain but save the broth.

3. Heat the sesame oil in a frying pan and sauté the tofu, turning often to brown all sides. (Or place on wooden skewers and grill with other vegetables.) Drain well on a piece of kitchen paper.

4. Combine all the sauce ingredients except the coriander in a food processor and process until smooth, adding the reserved broth as needed to create a gravy-like consistency. Heat through, then add the coriander.
5. Serve over rice and garnish with the coriander sprigs and lemon slices.

Serves 6 to 8

Prominent Tastes: *Pungent, Astringent*	
If you want to reduce	*eat*
VATA	SOME
PITTA	MORE
KAPHA	SOME

Vegetable Chow Mein

◆

When you master Chinese cooking, the variations are endless.

40 minutes to prepare

1 leek, washed thoroughly *(pungent, sweet)*

2 carrots *(sweet, pungent)*

2 courgettes *(sweet)*

2 celery stalks *(bitter, astringent)*

1 garlic clove, minced *(all but sour)*

5cm/2in piece of fresh root ginger, peeled and minced or grated *(pungent, sweet)*

2 tablespoons dark toasted sesame oil *(sweet)*

200g/7oz sliced water chestnuts, optional *(sweet)*

110g/4oz mushrooms, sliced *(sweet, astringent)*

450g/1 lb firm tofu, drained and cut into 3cm/1in pieces *(sweet, astringent)*

450g/1 lb fresh Chinese rice or chow mein noodles *(sweet)*

2 tablespoons finely chopped fresh coriander *(pungent)*

1. Slice the leek, carrots, courgettes and celery into bite-sized pieces.
2. In a wok or frying pan, sauté the garlic and ginger in 1 tablespoon hot sesame oil. Keeping the temperature high, add the leek, carrots, courgettes, celery and optional water chestnuts. Stir-fry quickly, then remove from the pan.
3. Adding a little more oil if necessary, stir-fry the mushrooms and tofu until browned on all sides. Remove from the pan and drain well.
4. While you are stir-frying, cook the noodles according to packet instructions. Rinse well in cold water until completely cool and drain well. Pan-fry in a hot, lightly oiled wok or frying pan until browned. (Constant stirring and scraping is necessary to prevent the noodles from sticking to the bottom of the pan.)
5. Toss the vegetables, coriander and noodles together and serve.

Serves 4 to 6

Prominent Tastes: *Sweet, Pungent*	
If you want to reduce	*eat*
VATA	SOME
PITTA	SOME
KAPHA	SOME

Vegetable Tofu Crustless Pie

◆

*This takes just a few minutes to prepare and is great
for a quick dinner after work.*

50 minutes to prepare

1 large leek, washed, cut into
pieces, and washed again
(pungent, sweet)

110g/4oz sliced carrots *(sweet,
pungent)*

450g/1 lb spinach *(bitter)*

110g/4oz toasted pine nuts *(sweet)*

450g/1 lb firm tofu *(sweet,
astringent)*

2 tablespoons soy sauce *(astringent,
salty)*

1 teaspoon tarragon *(pungent)*

⅛ teaspoon grated nutmeg
(pungent, astringent)

4 eggs *(sweet)*

60g/2oz dry bread crumbs *(sweet)*

2 tablespoons sesame seeds *(sweet)*

1. Preheat the oven to 200°C/400°F/gas mark 6.
2. Place the leek, carrots, spinach, pine nuts and tofu, one kind at a time, in a food processor and process until finely ground or chopped.
3. In a dry nonstick pan, sauté the leek-carrot-spinach mixture for 2 minutes. Combine with all the remaining ingredients except the sesame seeds.
4. Pour into a lightly oiled 23 × 30cm/9 × 12in baking dish. Sprinkle with the sesame seeds and bake, uncovered, for 30 minutes.

Serves 6 to 8

Prominent Tastes: *Sweet, Pungent, Astringent*	
If you want to reduce	*eat*
VATA	MORE
PITTA	SOME
KAPHA	LESS

Vegetable Paneer Tart

◆

Different combinations of vegetables make this dish uniquely satisfying to each dosha.

45 minutes to prepare

770g/1¾ lb mixed vegetables, such as 2 leeks *(pungent, sweet)*, 1 broccoli floret *(bitter, astringent)*, 2 celery sticks *(bitter, astringent)*, 60g/2oz green beans *(sweet, astringent)*, ½ yellow pepper *(sweet, astringent)*, 230g/8oz mushrooms *(sweet, astringent)*, or 40g/5oz peas *(sweet, astringent)*

2 tablespoons ghee or oil *(sweet)*

110g/4oz Paneer cheese (page 168) *(sweet, sour)*

2 eggs *(sweet)*

Pinch of tarragon *(pungent)*

Pinch of sea salt *(salty)*

2 tablespoons soy sauce *(astringent, salty)*

1 recipe Pastry Dough (recipe follows)

30g/1oz bread crumbs *(sweet)*

1. Preheat the oven to 200°C/400° F/gas mark 6.
2. Chop all the vegetables except the peas into small pieces. In a frying pan, sauté all the vegetables in ghee or oil until tender.
3. Mix with the cheese, eggs, tarragon, salt and soy sauce. Pour into the pastry shell and sprinkle with the bread crumbs.
4. Bake for 40 minutes, until the centre of the tart is firm and the bread crumbs are golden.

PASTRY DOUGH

450g/1 lb organic unbleached plain white flour *(sweet, astringent)*

½ teaspoon sea salt *(salty)*

230g/8oz cold, unsalted butter, cut into pieces *(sweet)*

110g/4oz lard *(sweet)*

170–230ml/6–8 fl oz ice-cold orange juice *(sweet, sour)*

1. Place the flour, salt, butter and lard in the food processor and process until mealy. Slowly pour in the orange juice until the dough begins to hold together.
2. Wrap the dough in clingfilm and refrigerate for 30 minutes.
3. Roll out half of the dough on a floured surface to form a shell. Place in a 25cm/10in flan tin. The remaining dough can be stored in the refrigerator for several days.

Serves 4 to 6

Prominent Tastes: *Sweet, Astringent, Bitter*	
If you want to reduce	*eat*
VATA	SOME
PITTA	MORE
KAPHA	LESS

Vegetable Strudel

◆

The vegetables you use in this dish can be determined by your doshic requirements.

45 minutes to 1 hour to prepare

770g/1¾ lb mixed fresh vegetables, such as potatoes *(astringent)*, carrots *(sweet, pungent)* and courgettes *(sweet)*, cut into bite-sized pieces

1 tablespoon ghee *(sweet)*

225g/8oz organic frozen corn *(sweet)*

225g/8oz organic frozen peas *(sweet, astringent)*

2 tablespoons vegetable bouillon powder *(all)*

½ teaspoon thyme *(pungent)*

½ tablespoon tarragon *(pungent)*

½ tablespoon oregano *(pungent)*

½ tablespoon rosemary *(pungent, bitter)*

¼ teaspoon sea salt *(salty)*

2 tablespoons soy sauce *(astringent, salty)*

1 tablespoon cornflour *(sweet)*

500g/17¾oz frozen puff pastry, thawed *(sweet)*

Egg glaze made from 1 egg beaten with 1 tablespoon water *(sweet)*

Sesame seeds *(sweet)*

Dried parsley *(pungent, astringent)*

1. In a large frying pan, sauté the fresh vegetables in the ghee until tender. Add the frozen corn and peas, the bouillon powder, the herbs, the salt, soy sauce and the cornflour and toss. Cool.
2. Preheat the oven to 200°C/400° F/gas mark 6.
3. On a floured surface, roll out the defrosted puff pastry into a large rectangle. Place the cooled filling onto the pastry at one end and fold over the sides. Moisten the edges with water. Roll up into a burrito-like shape. Brush with the egg glaze and sprinkle with sesame seeds and dried parsley.
4. Bake about 45 minutes. Serve immediately.

Serves 6 to 8

Prominent Taste: *Balanced*	
If you want to reduce	eat
VATA	SOME
PITTA	SOME
KAPHA	SOME

❦ Baked Winter Squash with Wild Rice-Cranberry Stuffing

◆

Warm and filling, this can be put together in the morning and baked before dinner.

1½ hours to prepare

2 medium winter squash, such as kabocha, acorn or butternut *(sweet)*

230ml/8 fl oz orange juice *(sweet, sour)*

200g/7oz wild rice *(sweet)*

Pinch of sea salt *(salty)*

110g/4oz toasted pine nuts *(sweet)*

40g/1½oz dried cranberries *(astringent, sweet)*

1 tablespoon dried minced onion *(pungent, sweet)*

1 teaspoon grated orange zest *(bitter)*

1 tablespoon soy sauce *(astringent, salty)*

1 teaspoon dried sage *(pungent, astringent)*

2 tablespoons bread crumbs *(sweet)*

1. Preheat the oven to 180°C/350°F/gas mark 4.
2. Split the squash in half lengthways. Remove the seeds and stringy pulp with a large spoon. Place the squash halves in a baking dish with the orange juice, cover and bake for 45 minutes, until cooked through but still firm. Reserve the juice.
3. Bring 470ml/16 fl oz of water to a boil. Add the rice and salt and simmer for 30 to 40 minutes, until the rice is fluffy.

4. Combine the rice with all the remaining ingredients except the bread crumbs. Add the reserved orange juice. Mound this mixture in the hollow of the squash and sprinkle with the bread crumbs.

5. Bake for 30 minutes, until heated through and the bread crumbs are browned.

Serves 4

Prominent Tastes: *Sweet, Pungent, Astringent*	
If you want to reduce	eat
VATA	SOME
PITTA	SOME
KAPHA	LESS

Veggie Burgers

◆

The recipe for these uniquely satisfying patties makes enough for a party.

1½ hours to prepare

140g/5oz pearl barley *(sweet)*

140g/5oz brown lentils *(sweet, astringent)*

140g/5oz basmati rice *(sweet)*

170g/6oz grated carrots *(sweet, pungent)*

110g/4oz chopped celery *(bitter, astringent)*

60ml/2 fl oz vegetable oil plus additional for frying *(sweet)*

30g/1oz sunflower seeds *(sweet)*

1 tablespoon chopped fresh basil or 1 teaspoon dried *(pungent)*

2 teaspoons chopped fresh thyme or 1 teaspoon dried *(pungent)*

2 teaspoons chopped fresh oregano or 1 teaspoon dried *(pungent)*

Sea salt *(salty)*

Pepper *(pungent)*

4 large eggs, beaten *(sweet)*

7 tablespoons flour *(sweet)*

1. Bring 700ml/1¼ pints of water to a boil in a heavy pot. Stir in the barley, lentils and rice. Cover and cook until the grains are tender, about 40 minutes. Drain, transfer to a large bowl, cool completely.
2. In a frying pan, sauté the carrots and celery in the 50ml/2 fl oz of vegetable oil until tender, about 12 minutes. Add to the grains and let cool. Mix in the seasonings and salt and pepper to taste.
3. Stir the beaten eggs and flour into the mixture. Press 60g/2oz of the mixture between the palms of your hands to form patties.
4. Heat additional oil in a large heavy frying pan. Add patties in batches and cook until golden brown, about 5 minutes on each side. Serve on wholemeal buns.

Serves 12 to 14

Prominent Tastes: *Sweet, Pungent*	
If you want to reduce	*eat*
VATA	MORE
PITTA	SOME
KAPHA	LESS

Cosmic Curry

◆

Choose your own vegetables to make this dish uniquely yours.

45 minutes to prepare

1 sweet potato, peeled and cubed (leave out for **Kaphas**) *(sweet)*

110g/4oz diced carrots *(sweet, pungent)*

60g/2oz diced leeks, washed well *(pungent, sweet)*

60g/2oz diced cauliflower *(sweet, astringent)*

2 tablespoons ghee *(sweet)*

3 plum tomatoes, quartered *(sweet, sour)*

450g/1 lb spinach, washed and stemmed *(bitter)*

340ml/12 fl oz coconut milk *(sweet)*

1 tablespoon grated fresh root ginger *(pungent, sweet)*

1 tablespoon ground cumin seeds *(pungent)*

2 teaspoons ground coriander *(pungent, bitter)*

1 teaspoon cinnamon *(pungent, bitter)*

½ teaspoon turmeric *(bitter, pungent, astringent)*

Pinch ground cardamom *(pungent, sweet)*

1 tablespoon lemon grass *(pungent, sour)*

4 tablespoons soy sauce *(astringent, salty)*

1 tablespoon vegetable bouillon powder *(all)*

Pinch of sea salt *(salty)*

450g/1 lb cooked basmati rice *(sweet)*

1. In a frying pan, sauté the sweet potato, carrots, leeks and cauliflower in 1 tablespoon ghee for 10 minutes. Add the tomatoes and spinach and cook until tender, about 3 minutes.
2. Add the remaining ingredients except rice with 230ml/8 fl oz water and bring to a quick boil. Turn off the heat and let stand until ready to serve.
3. Reheat, if necessary, and serve over basmati rice.

Serves 6 to 8

Prominent Taste: *Balanced*	
If you want to reduce	*eat*
VATA	MORE
PITTA	MORE
KAPHA	LESS

COSMIC CURRY ENCHILADAS

◆

Using lots of spices and vegetables, these are good for every dosha.

1 hour to prepare

1 sweet potato, peeled and cubed (leave out for **Kaphas**) *(sweet)*

110g/4oz diced carrots *(sweet, pungent)*

110g/4oz chopped leeks, washed well *(pungent)*

110g/4oz diced cauliflower *(sweet, astringent)*

2 tablespoons ghee *(sweet)*

3 plum tomatoes, quartered *(sweet)*

450g/1 lb spinach, washed and stemmed *(bitter)*

1 tablespoon grated fresh root ginger *(pungent)*

1 tablespoon ground cumin seeds *(pungent)*

2 teaspoons ground coriander *(pungent, sweet)*

1 teaspoon cinnamon *(pungent, sweet)*

½ teaspoon turmeric *(bitter, pungent, astringent)*

2 pinches ground cardamom *(pungent, sweet)*

1 tablespoon lemon grass *(pungent, sour)*

4 tablespoons soy sauce *(astringent, salty)*

1 tablespoon vegetable bouillon powder *(all)*

Pinch of sea salt *(salty)*

340ml/12 fl oz coconut milk *(sweet)*

10 to 12 Wholemeal Chapattis (page 146) *(sweet)*

2 tablespoons dried parsley or ground coriander *(pungent, astringent)*

1. Preheat the oven to 180°C/350°F/gas mark 4.
2. In a large frying pan, sauté the sweet potato, carrots, leeks and cauliflower in 1 tablespoon ghee for 10 minutes. Add the tomatoes and spinach and cook until tender, about 3 minutes.
3. Mix the herbs, spices, soy sauce, vegetable bouillon powder, salt, coconut milk and 110ml/4 fl oz of water in a bowl. Set aside 230ml/ 8 fl oz. Mix the rest into the vegetables.
4. Roll into the chapattis, place in an oiled baking dish and cover with the remaining sauce. Sprinkle with parsley or coriander and bake for 20 minutes, or until bubbly.

Serves 6 to 8

Prominent Taste: *Balanced*	
If you want to reduce	*eat*
VATA	MORE
PITTA	MORE
KAPHA	SOME

Side Dishes

◆

Our side dishes offer interest and balance to your main event.

BARLEY PILAF

BRAISED FENNEL

COCONUT BEANS

CRACKED WHEAT PILAF

CUMINY GREENS

GLAZED CARROTS

LEEKS AND LIMAS

MINTED PEA SOUFFLÉ

MINTED RICE AND PEAS

ORANGE ALMOND RICE

ORANGE ALMOND
SPINACH

POTATO HASH

QUINOA PILAF

ROASTED MUSTARD
POTATOES

SAFFRON RICE

SWEET SWEET POTATOES

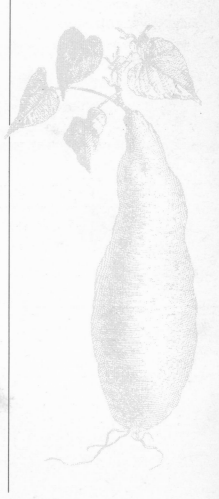

♥Barley Pilaf

◆

*This is best for **Pitta** and **Kapha**.*

1 hour to prepare

½ teaspoon sea salt *(salty)*

200g/7oz barley *(sweet)*

¼ teaspoon ghee or olive or sunflower oil *(sweet)*

30g/1oz diced celery *(bitter, astringent)*

30g/1oz diced carrots *(sweet, pungent)*

40g/1½oz peas *(sweet, astringent)*

1 tablespoon soy sauce *(astringent, salty)*

1 tablespoon vegetable bouillon powder *(all)*

1. In a saucepan, bring 950ml/1¾ pints of water and the salt to a boil. Add the barley and simmer for 45 minutes, or until the barley is soft and the water is absorbed.
2. In a frying pan, heat the ghee or oil to the smoking point. Add the vegetables and sauté 5 minutes. Add to the cooked barley with the soy sauce and vegetable bouillon powder. Let stand 5 minutes before serving.

Serves 4 to 6

Prominent Tastes:	*Sweet, Astringent*
If you want to reduce	eat
VATA	SOME
PITTA	MORE
KAPHA	MORE

♥BRAISED FENNEL

◆

The fennel bulb is balanced with a buttery, oniony taste.

1 hour to prepare

3 fennel bulbs, stems removed *(pungent, sweet)*

1 teaspoon ghee *(sweet)*

180ml/6 fl oz orange juice *(sweet, sour)*

Sea salt *(salty)*

Pepper *(pungent)*

1. Cut the fennel bulbs in half.
2. Melt the ghee in a frying pan. Place the fennel bulbs, cut sides down, in the pan and sauté, covered, about 10 minutes, until golden. Add the orange juice, salt and pepper and continue to cook for an additional 30 minutes, or until the liquid is absorbed and the fennel is soft.

Serves 2 to 4

Prominent Tastes: *Pungent, Sweet*	
If you want to reduce	eat
VATA	SOME
PITTA	SOME
KAPHA	SOME

Coconut Beans

◆

This is our version of an Indian speciality called Poriyal.

20 minutes to prepare

1 teaspoon olive or sunflower oil or ghee *(sweet)*

3 teaspoons brown mustard seeds *(pungent)*

3 teaspoons cumin seeds *(pungent)*

1.4kg/3 lbs green beans, finely chopped *(sweet, astringent)*

Sea salt *(salty)*

½ teaspoon asafoetida (hing) *(pungent)*

6 tablespoons dessicated coconut *(sweet)*

1 tablespoon ghee *(sweet)*

1. In a heavy saucepan, heat the oil or ghee to the smoking point. Add the mustard seeds and cumin seeds. When the seeds sputter, add the beans, salt, hing and 60ml/2 fl oz of water. Cover and simmer over low heat until the beans are tender.

2. Add the coconut and 1 tablespoon of ghee; mix well.

Serves 4 to 6

Prominent Tastes: *Sweet, Pungent*	
If you want to reduce	eat
VATA	SOME
PITTA	LESS
KAPHA	SOME

♥CRACKED WHEAT PILAF

◆

20 minutes to prepare

¼ teaspoon ghee or olive or sunflower oil *(sweet)*

130g/4½oz cracked wheat *(sweet, astringent)*

½ teaspoon sea salt *(salty)*

30g/1oz diced celery *(bitter, astringent)*

30g/1oz diced carrots *(sweet, pungent)*

40g/1½oz peas *(sweet, astringent)*

1 tablespoon dried minced onion *(pungent, sweet)*

1 tablespoon soy sauce *(astringent, salty)*

1 tablespoon vegetable bouillon powder *(all)*

1. In a frying pan, heat the ghee or oil to the smoking point. Add the cracked wheat and salt. Stirring frequently, brown the wheat.
2. Add the celery, carrots and peas and sauté 5 minutes.
3. Add the onion, soy sauce, vegetable bouillon powder and 470ml/ 16 fl oz of water. Simmer 15 minutes. Let stand 5 minutes before serving.

Serves 4 to 6

Prominent Tastes: *Sweet, Pungent, Astringent*	
If you want to reduce	*eat*
VATA	SOME
PITTA	SOME
KAPHA	LESS

CUMINY GREENS

◆

Use any combination of greens for a satisfying, pacifying dish.

20 minutes to prepare

1 teaspoon olive oil or ghee *(sweet)*

3 teaspoons brown mustard seeds *(pungent)*

3 teaspoons cumin seeds *(pungent)*

½ teaspoon minced garlic *(all but sour)*

1.4kg/3 lbs greens, such as kale, Swiss chard or spinach *(bitter)*

Pinch of sea salt *(salty)*

1. In a heavy saucepan, heat the oil. Add the mustard seeds, cumin seeds and garlic. When the seeds sputter, add the greens, salt and 60ml/2 fl oz of water.
2. Cover and simmer over low heat until the greens are tender, about 15 minutes.

Serves 4 to 6

Prominent Tastes: *Bitter, Pungent*	
If you want to reduce	*eat*
VATA	SOME
PITTA	SOME
KAPHA	MORE

GLAZED CARROTS

◆

20 minutes to prepare

230g/8oz cleaned, chopped baby
carrots *(sweet, pungent)*
½ teaspoon ghee *(sweet)*

1 tablespoon soy sauce *(astringent,
salty)*
1 teaspoon maple syrup *(sweet)*

1. Blanch the carrots by immersing in boiling water for 5 minutes. Remove and rinse immediately in cold water to stop the cooking and retain the colour. Drain.
2. In a frying pan, heat the ghee to the smoking point. Add the carrots and cook 3 minutes, until slightly browned. Add soy sauce and maple syrup. Toss and serve.

Serves 4 to 6

Prominent Tastes: *Sweet, Astringent*	
If you want to reduce	*eat*
VATA	SOME
PITTA	SOME
KAPHA	LESS

LEEKS AND LIMAS

◆

1 hour, 20 minutes to prepare

200g/7oz dried lima beans *(sweet, astringent)*

½ teaspoon salt *(salty)*

1 teaspoon olive oil *(sweet)*

2 large leeks, diced and well washed *(pungent, sweet)*

2 medium courgettes, diced *(sweet)*

6 plum tomatoes, diced *(sweet, sour)*

1 tablespoon soy sauce *(astringent, salty)*

1 tablespoon vegetable bouillon powder *(all)*

¼ teaspoon cardamom *(pungent, sweet)*

½ teaspoon cumin *(pungent)*

1. In a saucepan, bring 950ml/1¾ pints of water to a boil. Add the lima beans and salt and simmer for 1 hour.
2. In a large frying pan, bring the oil to the smoking point. Sauté the leeks and courgettes for 5 minutes. Add the tomatoes and heat through.
3. Add the remaining ingredients and toss. Let stand 10 minutes before serving.

Serves 4 to 6

Prominent Tastes: *Sweet, Astringent*	
If you want to reduce	*eat*
VATA	SOME
PITTA	MORE
KAPHA	MORE

Minted Pea Soufflé

◆

Frozen peas can be used in winter,
but fresh peas are so aromatic and sweet!

40 minutes to prepare

½ teaspoon ghee *(sweet)*

2 medium shallots, chopped *(pungent)*

450g/1 lb fresh peas *(sweet, astringent)*

2 eggs, beaten *(sweet)*

110g/4oz ricotta or Paneer cheese (page 168) *(sweet)*

Pinch of tarragon *(pungent)*

2 teaspoons chopped fresh mint or 1 teaspoon dried *(pungent)*

Pinch of sea salt *(salty)*

2 tablespoons soy sauce *(astringent, salty)*

30g/1oz fresh bread crumbs *(sweet)*

1. Preheat the oven to 180°C/350°F/gas mark 4.
2. In a frying pan, heat the ghee to the smoking point. Sauté the shallots until tender. Add the peas and continue to cook for 3 minutes. Process in a food processor until the peas and shallots are puréed.
3. Mix well with the eggs, cheese, tarragon, mint, salt and soy sauce. Pour into an oiled casserole dish and sprinkle with the bread crumbs.
4. Bake for about 30 minutes, until firm and the bread crumbs are browned.

Serves 4 to 6

Prominent Taste: *Sweet*	
If you want to reduce	*eat*
VATA	MORE
PITTA	MORE
KAPHA	LESS

♥Minted Rice and Peas
◆

Mint and peas are a harmonious blend.

20 minutes to prepare

200g/7oz basmati rice *(sweet)*
½ teaspoon sea salt *(salty)*
½ teaspoon ghee, optional *(sweet)*
140g/5oz cooked fresh or frozen
   organic peas *(sweet, astringent)*

1 tablespoon minced fresh mint or
½ tablespoon crushed dried mint
(pungent)

1. In a saucepan, place the rice, 570ml/1 pint of water and salt. Bring to a boil and simmer about 15 minutes.
2. Add the remaining ingredients and toss gently.

Serves 4 to 6

Prominent Tastes: *Sweet, Astringent*	
If you want to reduce	*eat*
VATA	MORE
PITTA	MORE
KAPHA	LESS

♥Orange Almond Rice

◆

20 minutes to prepare

200g/7oz basmati rice *(sweet)*
Pinch of sea salt *(salty)*
1 tablespoon soy sauce *(astringent, salty)*
60ml/2 fl oz orange juice concentrate *(sweet, sour)*

¼ teaspoon orange zest *(bitter)*
2 tablespoons ground or toasted flaked almonds *(sweet, bitter)*
Dash of grated nutmeg *(pungent)*

1. In a saucepan, bring 470ml//16 fl oz of water to a boil. Add the rice and salt and simmer 15 minutes.
2. Add soy sauce, orange juice concentrate and orange zest. Toss.
3. Serve on plates, garnished with the almonds and nutmeg.

Serves 4 to 6

Prominent Tastes: *Sweet, Bitter*	
If you want to reduce	*eat*
VATA	MORE
PITTA	SOME
KAPHA	LESS

♥Orange Almond Spinach

◆

20 minutes to prepare

1.4kg/3 lbs spinach *(bitter)*
Pinch of sea salt *(salty)*
1 tablespoon soy sauce *(astringent, salty)*
60ml/2 fl oz orange juice concentrate *(sweet, sour)*

¼ teaspoon orange zest *(bitter)*
2 tablespoons ground or toasted flaked almonds *(sweet, bitter)*
Dash of grated nutmeg *(pungent, astringent)*

1. In a frying pan, bring 6 tablespoons of water to a boil. Add the spinach and salt to taste. Cook for 5 minutes, or until the spinach is just wilted. Don't overcook.
2. Add soy sauce, orange juice concentrate and orange zest. Toss.
3. Serve on plates, garnished with the almonds and nutmeg.

Serves 4 to 6

Prominent Tastes: *Bitter, Sweet*	
If you want to reduce	eat
VATA	SOME
PITTA	SOME
KAPHA	MORE

Potato Hash

◆

The flesh of the yellow potato gives a buttery texture to this dish.

25 minutes to prepare

340g/12oz diced yellow potatoes *(astringent)*

110g/4oz diced leeks, washed well *(pungent, sweet)*

110g/4oz red pepper *(sweet, astringent)*

140g/5oz fresh corn kernels *(sweet)*

1 tablespoon olive oil *(sweet)*

1 teaspoon dried thyme *(pungent)*

½ teaspoon dried tarragon *(pungent)*

Dash of sea salt *(salty)*

Dash of pepper *(pungent)*

3 tablespoons chopped fresh coriander *(pungent)*

1. Boil the potatoes in water to cover for 5 minutes. Drain well. Toss in a bowl with the rest of the ingredients.
2. Sauté the potato mixture in a lightly oiled frying pan until browned and crispy. Serve immediately.

Serves 4 to 6

Prominent Tastes: *Pungent, Astringent*	
If you want to reduce	*eat*
VATA	LESS
PITTA	SOME
KAPHA	MORE

♥Quinoa Pilaf

◆

*Quinoa is not actually a grain, although it is treated that way.
It's a relative of the spinach plant!*

20 minutes to prepare

230g/8oz quinoa *(sweet, astringent)*
½ teaspoon sea salt *(salty)*
1 tablespoon dried minced onion
(pungent, sweet)
1 tablespoon soy sauce *(astringent, salty)*

1 tablespoon vegetable bouillon
powder *(all)*
½ teaspoon ghee (optional) *(sweet)*

1. In a saucepan, bring 460ml/16 fl oz of water to a boil. Add the quinoa
   and salt and simmer for 15 minutes.
2. Add the onion, soy sauce and vegetable bouillon powder and the
   optional ghee. Let stand 5 minutes before serving.

Serves 4 to 6

Prominent Tastes: *Sweet, Astringent*	
If you want to reduce	*eat*
VATA	SOME
PITTA	MORE
KAPHA	SOME

Roasted Mustard Potatoes

◆

Serve this, warm or at room temperature, instead of potato salad.

1 hour to prepare

450g/1 lb yellow or red potatoes, diced *(astringent)*

1 tablespoon olive oil *(sweet)*

1 tablespoon dried minced onion *(pungent, sweet)*

Pinch of sea salt

1 tablespoon soy sauce *(astringent, salty)*

1 tablespoon Dijon mustard *(pungent)*

1 tablespoon honey (optional) *(sweet)*

1. Preheat the oven to 200°C/400° F/gas mark 6.
2. Toss the potatoes in the oil, onion, salt and soy sauce. Place in a lightly oiled baking dish. Cover with foil and roast for 30 to 40 minutes.
3. Remove the foil, toss and continue roasting for an additional 15 minutes, until the potatoes are browned. Toss with the Dijon mustard. Honey may be added, if desired.

Serves 6 to 8

Prominent Tastes: *Astringent, Pungent*	
If you want to reduce	*eat*
VATA	LESS
PITTA	SOME
KAPHA	SOME

♥ SAFFRON RICE

◆

This is great with curries or green vegetables.

20 minutes to prepare

200g/7oz basmati rice *(sweet)*
½ teaspoon sea salt *(salty)*
⅛ teaspoon saffron threads
  (pungent)

1 teaspoon warm water
1 teaspoon ground cumin *(pungent)*

In a saucepan, place the rice, 570ml/1 pint of water and salt. While bringing to a boil, mix the saffron in the warm water and add to the rice with the cumin. Cook about 15 minutes.

Serves 4 to 6

Prominent Tastes: *Sweet, Pungent*	
If you want to reduce	eat
VATA	SOME
PITTA	SOME
KAPHA	LESS

Sweet Sweet Potatoes

◆

This is a favourite at the Center.
*Everyone loves it, although **Kaphas** should eat less.*

20 minutes to prepare

1 tablespoon ghee *(sweet)*

6 sweet potatoes, peeled and diced *(sweet)*

2 tablespoons soy sauce *(astringent, salty)*

2 tablespoons maple syrup *(sweet)*

2 tablespoons desiccated coconut *(sweet)*

1 teaspoon cumin *(pungent)*

1. In a large frying pan, heat the ghee to the smoking point. Sauté the sweet potatoes until tender and browned, about 10 minutes, stirring frequently with a spatula.
2. Remove from heat, toss with the remaining ingredients, and serve warm.

Serves 6 to 8

Prominent Taste: *Sweet*	
If you want to reduce	*eat*
VATA	MORE
PITTA	MORE
KAPHA	LESS

BREAD

◆

Bread is the all-time comfort food. Everyone loves bread, in all its shapes, sizes and guises. The variety of breads is unlimited and includes yeasted breads, flatbread, chapattis, focaccia, pizza dough, muffins and quick breads. In every culture, some form of bread goes with the meal.

With the advent of bread machines, much of the meditative quality of mixing and kneading bread is lost. The human touch through loving hands contributes wholeness and nourishment to the bread, and brings personal satisfaction to the baker.

Allow yourself time to enjoy the experience of kneading bread, dusting your hands with flour, shaping the loaves, and watching them rise in warm places. Your friends and family will appreciate your effort when they are greeted by the aromas of the warm, crusty loaves you pull from the oven.

Some dietary systems recommend avoiding all white bread, but when scattered throughout your week of menus with wholemeal or other whole grain recipes, white bread offers satisfaction to your palate and comfort to your soul. We recommend baking your white bread with organic unbleached strong flour, and wheat breads with organic wholemeal flour, fine if possible, and other whole ingredients. Vary the breads throughout the week just as you vary your vegetables and grains.

ANADAMA BREAD

CINNAMON RAISIN
BREAD

FOCACCIA

DARK DATE-NUT LOAF

FOUGASSE

FRENCH BREAD

GINGER-TREACLE
MUFFINS

OATMEAL MUFFINS

GOODY MUFFINS

ITALIANATE MUFFINS

NAAN

PITTA BREAD

SPELT BREAD

WHOLEMEAL
CHAPATTIS

Anadama Bread

◆

This early-American favourite uses whole grain flour and cornmeal for a rich, hearty flavour. Serve with Vegetable Barley Casserole (page 97) for a warm, wholesome lunch.

2 hours to prepare

1 sachet (7g/¼oz) fast acting dried yeast

230ml/8 fl oz lukewarm water

1 tablespoon soft butter, ghee or oil *(sweet)*

60ml/2 fl oz black treacle *(sweet)*

80g/2½oz cornmeal *(sweet)*

½ teaspoon sea salt *(salty)*

110g/4oz organic unbleached strong white flour *(sweet, astringent)*

230g/8oz organic wholemeal flour *(sweet, astringent)*

1. In a large bowl, dissolve the yeast in the water. Add the butter, ghee or oil with the treacle and cornmeal; stir to dissolve. Add the salt and flour, adding more flour if necessary, until the dough comes away from the sides of bowl as you mix. Knead in the bowl for about 5 minutes.

2. Cover and let rise until double, about an hour. Set near a warm stove or oven to quicken the rising process. Roll the dough out onto a floured surface. Knock back with your hand and divide into 2 equal-sized balls. Set aside for 10 minutes.

3. Preheat the oven to 190°C/375°F/gas mark 5.

4. Place the loaves into lightly oiled 450g/1 lb loaf tins and let rise again until double. Brush with water and make a cut down the middle of the loaves with a sharp knife. Place on the middle rack of the oven over a steaming pan of hot water, which you have placed on the bottom of the oven. The loaves are done when you hear a hollow sound when tapping lightly with your finger, 40 to 50 minutes. Cool on racks.

Makes 2 loaves

Prominent Taste: *Sweet*	
If you want to reduce	*eat*
VATA	SOME
PITTA	SOME
KAPHA	LESS

♥CINNAMON RAISIN BREAD

◆

Most recipes for cinnamon raisin bread use melted butter for adhering the filling to the insides of the dough. Here we use water for a non-fat bread treat.

2 to 4 hours to prepare

2 sachets (14g/½oz) fast acting dried yeast

2 tablespoons natural (unrefined) sugar *(sweet)*

470ml/16 fl oz lukewarm water

110g/4oz dried skimmed milk *(sweet)*

570–800g/1¼–1¾ lbs sifted organic unbleached strong white flour or a mixture of white and wholemeal

flour *(sweet, astringent)*

½ tablespoon sea salt *(salty)*

Filling

60ml/2 fl oz lukewarm water

170g/6oz raisins or currants *(sweet)*

2 tablespoons cinnamon *(pungent, bitter)*

1 tablespoon cardamom *(pungent, sweet)*

1. In a large bowl, dissolve the yeast and sugar in the water and let stand for 10 minutes. Stir in the milk, flour and salt. Knead in the bowl for about 5 minutes. Cover and let rise until double, 1 to 2 hours. Set it near a warm stove or oven to quicken the rising process.
2. Roll out onto a floured surface. Knock back with your hand and divide into 2 equal pieces.
3. Preheat the oven to 190°C/375°F/gas mark 5.

4. Dust the rolling surface with flour and roll out each piece into a 15 × 30cm/6 × 12in rectangle. Brush with the water, then sprinkle with the raisins, cinnamon and cardamom. Carefully roll up jelly roll style.

5. Place the loaves, seam sides down, in 2 lightly oiled 450g/1 lb loaf tins. Cover with a towel and let stand until the loaves rise above the top of the tins, 30 to 40 minutes.

6. Place a pan of hot water on the bottom of the oven. Place the tins on the middle rack and bake for 35 to 40 minutes, or until the loaves are golden brown. Cool on racks.

Makes 2 loaves

Prominent Taste: *Sweet*	
If you want to reduce	*eat*
VATA	MORE
PITTA	SOME
KAPHA	LESS

$\mathcal{F}$OCACCIA

◆

Much like pizza dough, this Italian favourite can be plain or generously covered with toppings.

2 hours to prepare

2 sachets (14g/½oz) fast acting dried yeast

470ml/16 fl oz lukewarm water

4 tablespoons olive oil *(sweet)*

570–800g/1¼–1¾ lbs organic unbleached strong white flour or organic wholemeal flour *(sweet, astringent)*

½ teaspoon sea salt *(salty)*

Topping possibilities: Olive oil, dried minced onion, coarse sea salt, caramelized red onion, rosemary, oregano

1. In a large bowl, dissolve the yeast in the lukewarm water. Add half of the oil, 500g/1¼ lb of flour and the salt. Mix until the dough comes away from the sides of the bowl, adding a little more flour, if necessary.
2. Dust the kneading surface with flour. Turn out the dough and knead for 8 to 10 minutes, or until smooth and elastic.
3. Transfer to a large oiled bowl and let rise until doubled, 40 to 70 minutes. Knock the dough back and turn out onto a floured surface. Cut into 2 equal pieces and let stand for 15 minutes.
4. Preheat the oven to 200°C/400°F/gas mark 6.
5. Lightly oil two 23 × 30cm/9 × 12in baking sheets. Place each piece on a baking sheet and, pressing out and away with the palms of your hands, cover the pan with the dough. At this point, the focaccia dough can be brushed with oil, sprinkled or spread with the desired topping, or left plain. Cover and let rise 25 minutes.
6. Place a pan of hot water in the bottom of the oven. Bake the focaccia on the middle rack for 10 to 15 minutes, or until golden brown. Serve warm.

Makes 2 loaves

Prominent Taste: *Sweet*	
If you want to reduce	*eat*
VATA	SOME
PITTA	SOME
KAPHA	LESS

Dark Date-Nut Loaf

◆

These dark, moist loaves make beautiful hostess presents or gifts for the Christmas holiday season.

1½ hours to prepare

110ml/4 fl oz boiling water

90g/3 oz currants *(sweet)*

90g/3 oz chopped date pieces *(sweet)*

1 teaspoon unsalted butter or ghee *(sweet)*

¾ teaspoon baking soda *(salty)*

60ml/2 fl oz black treacle *(sweet)*

110g/4oz organic unbleached strong white flour or wholemeal flour *(sweet, astringent)*

⅛ teaspoon sea salt *(salty)*

1 egg *(sweet)*

½ teaspoon vanilla essence *(sweet)*

30g/1oz chopped walnuts (optional) *(sweet)*

1. Preheat the oven to 180°C/350°F/gas mark 4.
2. In a bowl, pour the boiling water over the currants, dates, butter or ghee, and baking soda. Mix in the treacle. In a separate bowl, mix the flour and salt together; blend with the fruit mixture and the remaining ingredients.
3. Pour into an oiled 450g/1 lb loaf tin and bake for 1 hour, until crust forms. Remove from the tin to cool.

Makes 1 loaf

Prominent Taste: *Sweet*	
If you want to reduce	*eat*
VATA	MORE
PITTA	SOME
KAPHA	LESS

Fougasse

◆

These crusty flatbreads are great snacks or starters, or they can accompany any meal. Make the sponge the night before you wish to serve this yummy stuff. Make lots!

2 to 3 hours to prepare

Sponge

1 sachet (7g/½oz) fast acting dried yeast

120ml/4 fl oz lukewarm water

110g/4oz organic unbleached strong white flour or organic wholemeal flour *(sweet, astringent)*

1 sachet (7g/½oz) fast acting dried yeast

230ml/8 fl oz lukewarm water

2 tablespoons olive oil *(sweet)*

340–570g/12–20oz organic unbleached strong white flour or organic wholemeal flour *(sweet, astringent)*

½ teaspoon sea salt *(salty)*

140g/5oz cornmeal, for dusting pans *(sweet)*

1. Make the sponge: Dissolve the yeast in the lukewarm water. Add the flour and mix well. Cover and let stand overnight.
2. Using a wooden spoon, stir the sponge. Dissolve the yeast in the lukewarm water and add to the sponge with the oil, 340g/12oz of flour and salt. Mix until the dough comes away from the sides of the bowl, adding a little more flour, if necessary.
3. Dust the kneading surface with flour. Turn out the dough and knead for 8 to 10 minutes, or until smooth and elastic. Transfer to a large oiled bowl and let rise until doubled, 1 to 2 hours.
4. Knock back and turn out onto a floured surface. Cut into 8 equal pieces and shape each piece into rounds. Let stand for 15 minutes.
5. Preheat the oven to 200°C/400° F/gas mark 6.
6. Roll or stretch the rounds into ovals or triangles and place on baking sheets that have been dusted with cornmeal. Cover and let rise until doubled in size. Press with your thumbs in several places to create a textured surface and make several slashes with a sharp knife.

7. Place a pan of hot water in the bottom of the oven. Bake the fougasse on the middle rack for 10 to 15 minutes, or until golden brown. Serve warm.

Makes 8 pieces

Prominent Taste: *Sweet*	
If you want to reduce	*eat*
VATA	SOME
PITTA	SOME
KAPHA	LESS

♥ℱRENCH ℬREAD
◆

This bread is easy, great, warm – wow!

2 to 3 hours to prepare

2 sachets (14g/½oz) fast acting dried yeast

2 tablespoons natural (unrefined) sugar *(sweet)*

950ml/1¾ pints lukewarm water

900g/1¾ lb sifted organic unbleached strong white flour or a mixture of white and wholemeal flour *(sweet, astringent)*

1 teaspoon sea salt *(salty)*

1. In a large bowl, dissolve the yeast and sugar in 460ml/16 fl oz of the water. Let stand for 10 minutes. Stir in the flour and salt. Add just enough of the rest of the water to hold the dough together; it will form a soft, sticky dough.
2. Knead in the bowl for about 5 minutes, adding more flour, if necessary, to keep it from being too sticky. Cover and let rise until double, 1 to 2 hours. Set near a warm stove or oven to quicken the rising process.

3. Preheat the oven to 200°C/400°F/gas mark 6.
4. When the dough has risen, knock it back with your hand and divide into loaves: two 450g/1lb loaf tins. Clay will produce the best crust. Let rise again for 25 minutes, or until risen over the top of the tins.
5. Bake for 40 minutes on the middle rack over pans of hot water placed on the bottom of the oven, until browned and crusty.

Makes 1 large or 2 medium loaves

Prominent Taste: *Sweet*	
If you want to reduce	*eat*
VATA	SOME
PITTA	SOME
KAPHA	LESS

VARIATION: Add basil and/or oregano to the dry flour for an Italianate flavour.

Ginger-Treacle Muffins

◆

Fresh ginger gives these treats a pungent quality. Serve them for breakfast with Paneer cheese (page 168) and a warm cup of chai (page 167), or for dessert after a curry lunch.

30 minutes to prepare

60g/2oz butter or ghee, at room temperature *(sweet)*

60ml/2 fl oz black treacle *(sweet)*

2 large eggs *(sweet)*

280g/10 oz organic unbleached strong white flour or wholemeal flour *(sweet, astringent)*

1 teaspoon baking soda *(salty)*

¼ teaspoon sea salt *(salty)*

1 teaspoon cinnamon *(pungent, bitter)*

5cm/2in piece of fresh ginger, grated or finely chopped *(pungent, sweet)*

¼ teaspoon allspice *(pungent)*

¼ teaspoon cardamom *(pungent, sweet)*

230ml/8 fl oz boiling water

1. Preheat the oven to 190°C/375°F/gas mark 5.
2. In a bowl, mix together the butter or ghee, treacle and eggs until smooth. Blend in the remaining ingredients gently.
3. Pour the batter into lightly oiled muffin tins. Bake for 20 minutes. Cool on racks.

Makes 12 muffins

Prominent Tastes: *Sweet, Pungent*	
If you want to reduce	eat
VATA	MORE
PITTA	LESS
KAPHA	SOME

OATMEAL MUFFINS

◆

40 minutes to prepare

340g/12oz organic unbleached strong white flour *(sweet, astringent)*

200g/7oz rolled oats *(sweet)*

2 teaspoons baking powder *(salty)*

2 teaspoons bicarbonate of soda *(salty)*

1 teaspoon sea salt *(salty)*

90g/3oz natural (unrefined) sugar *(sweet)*

2 tablespoons cinnamon *(pungent, bitter)*

60ml/2 fl oz maple syrup *(sweet)*

450g/1 lb low-fat plain yoghurt *(sweet, sour)*

2 eggs *(sweet)*

110ml/4 fl oz skimmed milk *(sweet)*

3 tablespoons ghee *(sweet)*

1. Preheat the oven to 200°C/400° F/gas mark 6.
2. In a large bowl, sift together the dry ingredients. Combine with the remaining ingredients and blend gently.
3. Pour into 2 lightly oiled muffin tins. Bake for 25 minutes.

Makes 24 muffins

Prominent Taste: *Sweet*	
If you want to reduce	*eat*
VATA	MORE
PITTA	LESS
KAPHA	LESS

Goody Muffins

◆

These power-packed muffins start your day with a bang.
They contain all six tastes!

30 minutes to prepare

30g/1oz organic unbleached strong white flour *(sweet, astringent)*

170g/6oz wholemeal flour *(sweet, astringent)*

30g/1oz bran flakes *(sweet, astringent)*

30g/1oz rolled oats *(sweet)*

30g/1oz wheat germ *(sweet, astringent)*

30g/1oz ground sunflower seeds *(sweet, bitter)*

30g/1oz ground pine nuts *(sweet)*

60g/2oz dried skimmed milk *(sweet)*

1 tablespoon baking powder *(salty)*

¼ teaspoon sea salt *(salty)*

2 eggs *(sweet)*

230g/8oz low-fat plain yoghurt *(sour)*

60ml/2 fl oz sunflower oil *(sweet)* for **Pitta** and **Kapha** or safflower oil *(sweet, pungent)* for **Vata**

110g/4oz natural (unrefined) sugar *(sweet)*

40g/1½oz each:
chopped date pieces *(sweet)*
apricots *(sweet, sour)*
raisins or currants *(sweet)* (good for **Kapha,** leave out for **Vata**)
coconut *(sweet)*

1. Preheat the oven to 200°C/400°F/gas mark 6.
2. In a large bowl, combine the first 10 ingredients.
3. In a separate mixing bowl, blend the eggs, yoghurt, oil and sugar gently. Add the fruit and coconut. Fold in the other ingredients.
4. Pour the batter into a lightly oiled muffin tin. Bake 15 to 20 minutes. Cool on racks and serve warm or at room temperature.

Makes 12 muffins

Prominent Tastes: *All*	
If you want to reduce	*eat*
VATA	SOME
PITTA	SOME
KAPHA	SOME

Italianate Muffins

◆

*These savoury muffins are great with pasta or as an
accompaniment to salad.
For **Vatas** and **Pittas,** cheese may be added.*

30 minutes to prepare

230g/8oz organic unbleached strong
white flour *(sweet, astringent)*

1 tablespoon baking powder *(salty)*

½ teaspoon sea salt *(salty)*

¼ teaspoon dried oregano *(pungent)*

¼ teaspoon dried crumbled
rosemary *(pungent, bitter)*

¼ teaspoon dried thyme *(pungent)*

2 pinches crushed chillies *(pungent)*

2 eggs *(sweet)*

230ml/8 fl oz skimmed milk *(sweet)*

60ml/2 fl oz olive oil *(sweet)*

1 tablespoon natural (unrefined)
sugar *(sweet)*

1 garlic clove, minced *(all but sour)*

60g/2oz sun-dried tomatoes,
drained and chopped *(sweet, sour)*

110g/4oz grated Parmesan cheese,
optional *(sweet)*

1. Preheat the oven to 200°C/400°F/gas mark 6
2. In a large bowl, combine the first 7 ingredients.
3. In a separate mixing bowl, gently blend the eggs, milk, oil and sugar
   together. Add the garlic and sun-dried tomatoes. Fold in the other
   ingredients.

4. Pour the batter into a lightly oiled muffin tin. Bake 15 to 20 minutes. Cool on racks and serve warm or at room temperature.

Makes 12 muffins

Prominent Tastes: *All*	
If you want to reduce	eat
VATA	SOME
PITTA	SOME
KAPHA	SOME

♥ 𝒩AAN
◆

Don't have a tandoor oven in your back garden that reaches 700° F? That's okay. Using the highest temperature of your oven will work just as well for this bread, which is the Northern Indian equivalent of pitta (page 144) and fougasse (page 135).

40 to 50 minutes to prepare

1 sachet (7g/¼oz) fast acting dried yeast

110ml/4 fl oz lukewarm water

230g/8oz low-fat plain yoghurt *(sweet, sour)*

2 tablespoons vegetable oil *(sweet)*

340–570g/12–20oz organic unbleached strong white flour or organic wholemeal flour *(sweet, astringent)*

½ teaspoon sea salt *(salty)*

1. In a large bowl, dissolve the yeast in the lukewarm water. Add the yoghurt, oil, 340g/12oz of flour and the salt. Mix until the dough comes away from the sides of the bowl, adding a little more flour, if necessary. Don't add too much, though; this dough should be on the soft side.
2. Dust the kneading surface with flour. Turn out the dough and knead for 8 to 10 minutes, or until smooth and elastic. Transfer to a large oiled bowl and let rise until doubled, 30 to 40 minutes.
3. Knock the dough back and turn out onto a floured surface. Cut into 12 equal pieces and shape each piece into rounds. Let stand for 15 minutes.
4. Preheat the oven to 240°C/475°F.
5. Roll or stretch the rounds into 15cm/6in circles. Place a large baking sheet in the oven for 15 minutes. Open the oven door and quickly place the dough rounds, 2 at a time, onto the hot baking sheet. Bake 1 to 2 minutes on each side, until golden brown in places.
6. Cover the completed naans with a towel while baking others. These are best served warm; however, they can be cooled and refrigerated in plastic bags.

Makes 12 pieces

Prominent Taste: *Sweet*	
If you want to reduce	*eat*
VATA	SOME
PITTA	SOME
KAPHA	LESS

𝒫ITTA 𝓑READ

◆

1¹/₂ hours to prepare

1 sachet (7g/¼oz) fast acting dried
yeast
1 teaspoon natural (unrefined)
sugar *(sweet)*
280ml/½ pint lukewarm water
2 tablespoons olive oil *(sweet)*

1 teaspoon sea salt *(salty)*
340g/12oz sifted organic
unbleached strong white flour
plus more for rolling *(sweet,
astringent)*

1. In a large bowl, stir the yeast, sugar and half the water together. Let stand about 10 minutes, until bubbly. Add the remaining water, oil, salt and half the flour. Stir with a wooden spoon until blended. Add enough of the remaining flour, a little at a time, until the dough is no longer sticky.
2. Preheat the oven to 260°C/500°F/gas mark 10.
3. Turn the dough onto a floured board and cut into 6 equal pieces. Pat each into a 5mm/¼in-thick circle. Cover with a towel and let rest 30 minutes, until slightly puffed. Gather the balls into your hands one at a time and squeeze out the air. Roll into 5mm/¼in-thick circles again.
4. Lay the circles 2.5cm/1in apart on an ungreased baking sheet and bake on the lowest oven rack for 5 minutes. Move to a higher rack and bake an additional 2 minutes, until the circles are puffy and browned. Cool. Store in a plastic bag.

Makes 6 pittas

Prominent Taste: *Sweet*	
If you want to reduce	eat
VATA	MORE
PITTA	MORE
KAPHA	LESS

♥SPELT BREAD
◆

*Spelt, an ancient whole grain,
is often used for those with a wheat intolerance.*

2 to 3 hours to prepare

2 sachets (14g/½oz) fast acting
  dried yeast
2 tablespoons natural (unrefined)
  sugar *(sweet)*

950ml/1¾ pints lukewarm water
900g/2 lbs organic whole spelt flour
  (sweet, astringent)
½ tablespoon sea salt *(salty)*

1. In a large bowl, dissolve the yeast and sugar in 460ml/16 fl oz of the water. Let stand for 10 minutes.
2. Stir in the flour and salt. Add just enough of the rest of the water to hold the dough together; it will form a soft, sticky dough. Knead in the bowl for about 5 minutes.
3. Cover and let rise until double, 1 to 2 hours. Set near a warm oven to quicken the rising process.
4. Preheat the oven to 200°C/400°F/gas mark 6.
5. When the dough has risen, knock it back with your hand and divide into loaves: two 450g/1 lb loaf tins. Clay will produce the best crust. Let rise again for 25 minutes, or until risen over the top of the tins.
6. Bake for about 40 minutes, or until browned and crusty.

Makes 2 medium loaves or 1 large loaf

Prominent Taste: *Sweet*	
If you want to reduce	*eat*
VATA	MORE
PITTA	MORE
KAPHA	SOME

Wholemeal Chapattis

◆

This is a good yeastless bread.

1½ hours to prepare

250g/9oz wholemeal flour plus
  extra for rolling *(sweet, astringent)*
2 teaspoons sunflower oil *(sweet)*

Pinch of sea salt *(salty)*
280ml/½ pint lukewarm water

1. With a wooden spoon, mix the flour, oil and salt in a large bowl. Add the water and mix into a soft dough. Cover and let stand for 1 hour.
2. Moisten your hands with oil and make 25 to 30 small balls. Roll the balls in a small bowl of flour. Using a rolling pin, roll out on a floured surface to form 15cm/6in circles.
3. To cook chapattis, heat a large frying pan to medium. Cook each chapatti ½ minute on the first side, about 1 minute on the second side, until it puffs. Serve immediately or keep the chapattis covered until ready to use.

Makes 25 to 30 chapattis

Prominent Taste: *Sweet*	
If you want to reduce	*eat*
VATA	MORE
PITTA	MORE
KAPHA	LESS

DESSERTS

◆

Ancient seers knew that part of the glory of life was its sweetness. We think it's good to metabolize some sweetness every day.

Many of our desserts are low in fat, but some are not. Use your good judgement in the amount of dessert you eat and how often you eat it. Concentrated sweetness is best consumed at midday, when the digestive fire is strongest.

APRICOT BARS

BAKED APPLES

BAKLAVA

CHOCOLATE CHIP
COOKIES

DATE BARS

FRESH BLUEBERRY CAKE

FRENCH APPLE CAKE

GLAZED PEAR TART OR
POACHED PEARS

GINGER-TREACLE
COOKIES

MUESLI BARS

LEMON BARS

OUTRAGEOUS OATMEAL
COOKIES

PRUNE CAKE

Apricot Bars

◆

This recipe is good for all body types.

40 minutes to prepare

Crust | **Topping**

230g/8oz organic unbleached fine plain white flour *(sweet, astringent)*

4 tablespoons natural (unrefined) sugar *(sweet)*

60g/2oz cold unsalted butter *(sweet)*

60g/2oz organic unbleached fine plain white flour *(sweet, astringent)*

110g/4oz natural (unrefined) sugar *(sweet)*

1 teaspoon baking powder *(salty)*

1 teaspoon sea salt *(salty)*

2 eggs *(sweet)*

2 teaspoons vanilla essence *(sweet)*

310g/11oz chopped dried apricots *(sweet, sour)*

1. Preheat the oven to 180°C/350°F/gas mark 4.
2. Make the crust: In a food processor, mix the flour and sugar. Cut the cold butter into pieces and process with the flour and sugar until mealy. Press into the bottom of a 23 × 33cm/9 × 13in baking tin and bake 15 minutes.
3. Prepare the topping: In a small bowl, sift the flour, sugar, baking powder and salt. Add the remaining ingredients and stir until well mixed.
4. After cooling the crumb mixture, spread the topping over it and bake 20 minutes. Cool, cut into bars and serve warm or at room temperature.

Makes 12 to 18 bars

Prominent Taste: *Sweet*	
If you want to reduce	*eat*
VATA	SOME
PITTA	SOME
KAPHA	LESS

♥ BAKED APPLES

◆

Baked apples make a delicious breakfast or dessert.

45 minutes to prepare

2 Cox's or Granny Smith apples
  (sweet, astringent)
½ teaspoon ghee *(sweet)*
2 teaspoons ground pine nuts
  (sweet)
1 teaspoon cinnamon *(pungent)*

1 teaspoon maple syrup *(sweet)*
¼ teaspoon ground ginger
  (pungent)
60ml/2 fl oz unfiltered apple juice
  (sweet, astringent)

1. Preheat the oven to 200°C/400°F/gas mark 6.
2. Peel the top of the apples about ⅓ of the way down. Cut out a 2.5–3cm/1in piece of the centre cores.
3. Mix the ghee, nuts, cinnamon, maple syrup and ginger together and put in the well in the centre of the apples. Place in a baking dish with the apple juice, cover with foil and bake about 30 minutes. Uncover, baste with apple juice and bake until soft, about 15 more minutes.

Serves 2

Prominent Tastes: *Sweet, Astringent*	
If you want to reduce	*eat*
VATA	SOME
PITTA	SOME
KAPHA	SOME

ℬAKLAVA

◆

Made with maple syrup instead of honey, these treats are awesome.

1 hour to prepare

110g/4oz sunflower seeds *(sweet, bitter)*

60g/2oz pine nuts *(sweet)*

80g/2½oz roasted or blanched almonds *(sweet, bitter)*

170g/6oz raisins or currants *(sweet)*

40g/1½oz dessicated coconut *(sweet)*

60ml/2 fl oz maple syrup *(sweet)*

1 teaspoon vanilla essence *(sweet)*

4 sheets filo pastry *(sweet)*

Soft or melted ghee, for brushing *(sweet)*

Sesame seeds *(sweet)*

Maple syrup *(sweet)*

1. Preheat the oven to 180°C/350°F/gas mark 4.
2. In a food processor, combine the first 7 ingredients. Process for about 30 seconds, just long enough to chop up the ingredients but not so long as to pulverize them.
3. Spread the ghee over the filo pastry, stacking as you go. Remember, the more ghee you use, the more calories from fat are added. Just use barely enough to hold the filo sheets together.
4. Place the filling at one edge of the filo stack and roll up. Brush roll lightly with the ghee.
5. Cut into small squares and place on a baking tray. Sprinkle with sesame seeds and bake for about 25 minutes, or until golden. Drizzle with maple syrup. Cool completely before serving.

Makes 24 to 30 pieces

Prominent Taste: *Sweet*	
If you want to reduce	*eat*
VATA	MORE
PITTA	MORE
KAPHA	LESS

CHOCOLATE CHIP COOKIES

◆

Chocolate is not described in classic Ayurvedic texts, as it was not grown in India. Some scientists believe it has chemicals that mimic those produced by people in love.

1 hour to prepare

170g/6oz natural (unrefined) sugar
  (sweet)
170g/6oz butter, melted *(sweet)*
2 eggs *(sweet)*
1 tablespoon vanilla essence *(sweet)*
280g/10oz organic unbleached fine
  plain white flour or fine
  wholemeal flour *(sweet,*
  astringent)

1 teaspoon baking soda *(salty)*
¼ teaspoon sea salt *(salty)*
340g/12oz chocolate chips
  (pungent, bitter)
60g/2oz ground nuts of your choice
  (optional) *(sweet, bitter)*

1. Preheat the oven to 190°C/375°F/gas mark 5.
2. In a bowl, blend the first 4 ingredients. Add the flour, baking soda and salt and mix well.
3. Fold in the chocolate chips and add nuts, if desired.
4. Drop by teaspoonfuls onto a lightly oiled baking tray and bake for 8 to 10 minutes, until browned on the bottom but still soft in the middle. *Don't overcook. The cookies should be browned on the bottom only.*

Makes 60 cookies

Prominent Taste: *Sweet*	
If you want to reduce	eat
VATA	SOME
PITTA	SOME
KAPHA	LESS

Date Bars

◆

40 minutes to prepare

Crust

230g/8oz organic unbleached fine plain white flour *(sweet, astringent)*

40g/1½oz natural (unrefined) sugar *(sweet)*

60g/2oz cold unsalted butter *(sweet)*

Topping

90g/3oz flour *(sweet, astringent)*

90g/3oz natural (unrefined) sugar *(sweet)*

1 teaspoon baking powder *(salty)*

1 teaspoon sea salt *(salty)*

2 eggs *(sweet)*

2 teaspoons vanilla essence *(sweet)*

90g/3oz desiccated coconut *(sweet)*

340g/12oz chopped dates *(sweet)*

110g/4oz chopped pine nuts *(sweet)*

1. Preheat the oven to 180°C/350°F/gas mark 4.
2. Make the crust: in a food processor, mix the flour and sugar. Cut the cold butter into pieces and mix with the flour and sugar until mealy. Press into the bottom of a 23 × 33cm/9 × 13in baking tin and bake 15 minutes.
3. Make the topping: sift the flour, sugar, baking powder and salt into a bowl. Add the remaining ingredients and stir until well mixed.
4. After cooling the crumb mixture, spread the topping over it and bake 20 minutes. Cool, cut into bars and serve warm or at room temperature.

Makes 12 to 18 bars

Prominent Taste: *Sweet*	
If you want to reduce	*eat*
VATA	SOME
PITTA	SOME
KAPHA	LESS

Fresh Blueberry Cake

◆

1½ hours to prepare

Cake

900g/2 lbs fresh blueberries *(sweet, astringent)*

2 teaspoons cinnamon *(pungent, bitter)*

1 teaspoon nutmeg *(pungent, astringent)*

230g/8oz organic unbleached fine plain white flour *(sweet, astringent)*

2 teaspoons baking powder *(salty)*

90g/3oz natural (unrefined) sugar *(sweet)*

60ml/2 fl oz skimmed milk *(sweet)*

60ml/2 fl oz ghee *(sweet)*

4 eggs *(sweet)*

Topping

2 eggs *(sweet)*

60ml/2 fl oz ghee *(sweet)*

170g/6oz natural (unrefined) sugar *(sweet)*

2 teaspoons vanilla essence *(sweet)*

1. Preheat the oven to 160°C/325°F/gas mark 3. Lightly oil a 23 × 30cm/ 9 × 12in cake tin.
2. In a large bowl, toss the blueberries with the cinnamon and nutmeg; place in the cake tin. Put all the remaining cake ingredients in a bowl and beat well. Carefully pour the batter over the blueberries. Bake for about 45 minutes, or until golden brown.
3. Cream together the topping ingredients. Remove the cake from the oven, spoon the topping over it and return the cake to the oven for about 20 minutes, until the topping is browned and bubbly.

Makes 12 to 18 pieces

Prominent Tastes: *Sweet, Astringent*	
If you want to reduce	*eat*
VATA	SOME
PITTA	SOME
KAPHA	LESS

ℱrench 𝒜pple 𝒞ake

◆

*Cooked apples decrease **Vata**.*
This dessert goes well with a warm cup of chai (page 167).

1½ hours to prepare

Cake

900g/2 lbs Granny Smith or Cox's apples, cored and chopped *(sweet, astringent)*

2 teaspoons cinnamon *(pungent, bitter)*

1 teaspoon nutmeg *(pungent, astringent)*

230g/8oz organic unbleached fine plain white flour *(sweet, astringent)*

2 teaspoons baking powder *(salty)*

90g/3oz natural (unrefined) sugar *(sweet)*

60ml/2 fl oz skimmed milk *(sweet)*

60ml/2 fl oz ghee *(sweet)*

4 eggs *(sweet)*

Topping

2 eggs *(sweet)*

60ml/2 fl oz ghee *(sweet)*

170g/6oz natural (unrefined) sugar *(sweet)*

2 teaspoons vanilla essence *(sweet)*

1. Preheat the oven to 160°C/325°F/gas mark 3. Lightly oil a 23 × 30cm/ 9 × 12in cake tin.

2. In a large bowl, toss the chopped apples with the cinnamon and nutmeg and place in the cake tin. Put all the remaining cake ingredients in a bowl and beat well. Pour the batter over the apples and bake for about 45 minutes, or until golden brown.

3. Cream together the topping ingredients. Remove the cake from the oven, spoon the topping over it, and return the cake to the oven for about 20 minutes, until the topping is browned and bubbly.

Makes 12 to 18 pieces

Prominent Tastes: *Sweet, Astringent*	
If you want to reduce	*eat*
VATA	SOME
PITTA	SOME
KAPHA	SOME

GLAZED PEAR TART OR ♥POACHED PEARS

◆

When poached in cranberry juice, the pears turn a rich red.
*This is pacifying to **Vata** and **Pitta**.*

1¹/₂ hours to prepare tart
45 minutes to prepare poached pears

7 almost-ripe William pears *(sweet)*

950ml/1¾ pints cranberry juice *(sweet, sour)*

1 tablespoon crystallized ginger *(pungent, sweet)*

1 teaspoon cinnamon *(pungent, bitter)*

15g/½oz unsalted butter *(sweet)*

2 tablespoons natural (unrefined) sugar *(sweet)*

1 sheet frozen puff pastry, thawed (from 500g/17¾oz packet)

1 cup blackberry jam *(sweet, sour)*

1. Preheat the oven to 200°C/400°F/gas mark 6.
2. Poach the pears in the cranberry juice and spices for 25 to 35 minutes, until cooked but still firm. Remove from the pot and drain well.
3. Reduce the juice to a syrup. Add the butter and sugar.* Cool.
4. Cut the pears in half lengthways.

*Stop at this point for Poached Pears, spooning the syrup over the pears to serve.

5. Roll out the pastry dough according to package instructions to fit into a baking tray. Crimp the edges. Bake for 25 minutes or until golden. Cool. Spread with the blackberry jam. Arrange the pears, cut side down, on the pastry and pour the thickened syrup over the pears. Serve promptly.

Makes 10 to 12 pieces
Makes 7 pears

Prominent Taste: *Sweet*	
If you want to reduce	*eat*
VATA	MORE
PITTA	MORE
KAPHA	LESS

Ginger-Treacle Cookies

◆

1½ hours to prepare

130g/4½oz natural (unrefined)
sugar plus more for rolling *(sweet)*

110ml/4 fl oz ghee *(sweet)*

1 egg *(sweet)*

170g/6oz treacle *(sweet)*

2 teaspoons ground ginger
(pungent, sweet)

1 teaspoon ground cinnamon
(pungent, bitter)

2 teaspoons baking soda *(salty)*

½ teaspoon sea salt *(salty)*

310g/11oz organic unbleached fine
plain white flour *(sweet,
astringent)*

1. Preheat the oven to 160°C/325°F/gas mark 3.
2. In a bowl, blend the sugar and ghee well with a wooden spoon. Add the egg and treacle and mix well. Add the remaining ingredients and mix well. The mixture should be soft. Dust lightly with flour, wrap in cling-film and refrigerate for 30 minutes.
3. Shape into teaspoon-size balls and roll in the sugar. Place 3cm/1in apart on a lightly oiled baking tray, pressing flat with two fingers. Bake for about 10 minutes, or just until cracks appear on top. *The cookies should be browned on the bottom only.* Cool on a wire rack.

Makes 36 cookies

Prominent Tastes: *Sweet, Pungent*	
If you want to reduce	eat
VATA	SOME
PITTA	SOME
KAPHA	SOME

Muesli Bars

◆

This is a good breakfast item or snack.

40 minutes to prepare

40g/1½oz natural (unrefined) sugar *(sweet)*

110g/4oz unsalted butter, melted *(sweet)*

2 eggs *(sweet)*

1 tablespoon vanilla essence *(sweet)*

110g/4oz organic unbleached fine plain white flour *(sweet, astringent)*

1 teaspoon baking soda *(salty)*

¼ teaspoon sea salt *(salty)*

170g/6oz Muesli (page 174) *(sweet)*

40g/1½oz currants or raisins *(sweet)*

1. Preheat the oven to 190°C/375°F/gas mark 5
2. Blend the first 4 ingredients. Add the flour, baking soda and salt and mix well. Fold in the muesli and currants or raisins.
3. Press into a lightly oiled 23 × 30cm/9 × 12in baking dish. Bake for 10 to 15 minutes, until lightly brown but still soft in the middle. *Don't overcook.*

Makes 12 to 18 bars

Prominent Taste: *Sweet*	
If you want to reduce	*eat*
VATA	SOME
PITTA	SOME
KAPHA	LESS

ℒemon ℬars

◆

These are rich, but everyone wants this recipe.

45 minutes to prepare

Crust

230g/8oz organic unbleached fine
   plain white flour *(sweet, astringent)*
40g/1½oz natural (unrefined) sugar
   (sweet)
230g/8oz cold unsalted butter
   (sweet)

Topping

3 eggs *(sweet)*
110g/4oz unsalted butter, melted
   (sweet)
170g/6oz natural (unrefined) sugar
   (sweet)
110ml/4 fl oz lemon juice *(sour, astringent)*
Icing sugar, for sprinkling
   (optional) *(sweet)*

1. Preheat the oven to 180°C/350°F/gas mark 4.
2. Make the crust: in a food processor, mix the flour and sugar. Cut the cold butter into pieces and process with the flour and sugar until mealy. Press into the bottom of a 23 × 33cm/9 × 13in baking tin. Bake 15 minutes. Cool slightly.
3. In a food processor, combine the topping ingredients and process for 45 seconds. Pour evenly over the pastry.
4. Bake 25 minutes until set. Do not brown. Cool completely. Cut into small squares. Sprinkle with icing sugar, if desired.

Makes 18 to 30 bars

Prominent Taste: *Sweet*	
If you want to reduce	*eat*
VATA	MORE
PITTA	SOME
KAPHA	LESS

Outrageous Oatmeal Cookies

◆

Oh, boy!

45 minutes to prepare

130g/4½oz natural (unrefined) sugar *(sweet)*

170g/6oz unsalted butter, melted *(sweet)*

2 eggs *(sweet)*

1 tablespoon maple syrup *(sweet)*

230g/8oz organic unbleached fine plain white flour *(sweet, astringent)*

200g/7oz rolled oats *(sweet)*

170g/6oz chopped dates *(sweet)*

170g/6oz raisins *(sweet)*

90g/3oz desiccated coconut *(sweet)*

1 tablespoon cinnamon *(pungent, bitter)*

1 teaspoon baking soda *(salty)*

¼ teaspoon sea salt *(salty)*

1. Preheat the oven to 160°C/325°F/gas mark 3.
2. In a bowl, blend the first 4 ingredients. Add the remaining ingredients and mix well.
3. Drop by tablespoonfuls onto a lightly oiled baking tray and bake 8 to 10 minutes. *Don't overcook. The cookies should be browned on the bottom only.*

Makes 36 cookies

Prominent Taste: *Sweet*	
If you want to reduce	eat
VATA	MORE
PITTA	MORE
KAPHA	LESS

Prune Cake

◆

Serve this warm with yoghurt as part of a special breakfast.

1½ hours to prepare

340g/12oz chopped prunes *(sweet, sour)*

280ml/½ pint unfiltered apple juice *(sweet, astringent)*

2 teaspoons cinnamon *(pungent, bitter)*

1 teaspoon nutmeg *(pungent, astringent)*

340g/12oz organic unbleached fine plain white flour *(sweet, astringent)*

2 teaspoons baking powder *(salty)*

70g/6oz treacle *(sweet)*

60g/2oz low-fat plain yoghurt *(sweet, sour)*

60ml/2 fl oz ghee *(sweet)*

2 eggs *(sweet)*

1. Preheat the oven to 180°C/350°F/gas mark 4. Butter or oil a 23cm/9in-diameter cake tin.
2. In a saucepan, poach the prunes in the apple juice until quite soft, then mash in a food processor. Cool.
3. Combine the cinnamon, nutmeg, flour and baking powder in a mixing bowl.
4. In another bowl, blend the treacle, yoghurt, ghee and eggs. Add the mashed prunes, blending well. Add to the dry ingredients and mix.
5. Pour into the cake tin and bake for 1 hour, or until a knife inserted comes out clean. *Don't overcook.*

Makes 12 to 18 pieces

Prominent Taste: *Sweet*	
If you want to reduce	*eat*
VATA	SOME
PITTA	SOME
KAPHA	SOME

CONDIMENTS AND BEVERAGES

◆

This section covers important accessory foods to Ayurvedic cooking. Ghee, Paneer, lassi, chutneys and *churans* are easy to make and serve a wide range of culinary uses.

CHURANS	PANEER CHEESE
GHEE	CIRCUS SALSA
GINGER 'ELIXIR'	DATE-RAISIN CHUTNEY
LASSI	MANGO CHUTNEY
MORNING CHAI	TOMATO CHUTNEY

♥CHURANS
♦

*Making spice blends is a great way to personalize your foods.
Choose three or four spices and/or herbs that are appropriate for
each dosha. Then when seasoning vegetables, grains and pastas
you can rest assured that those seasonings will balance your
dosha. The possible choices are:*

10 minutes to prepare

Vata

cardamom, cumin, ginger,
cinnamon, salt, cloves, mustard
seed, black pepper

Kapha

turmeric, ginger, mustard, cayenne,
anise

Pitta

coriander, fennel, cumin, dill

GHEE

◆

Ghee, clarified butter, is an essential ingredient in Ayurvedic cooking. It is easy to digest and contributes to the absorption of nutrients. It can be purchased in most health food and Indian food shops. However, buying it is expensive. Once you make your own and discover how simple and delicious it is, you'll never buy it again.

45 minutes to prepare

450g/1 lb unsalted butter (organic,
   if possible) *(sweet)*

1. Cut the butter into cubes and cook over medium-high heat in a heavy saucepan until melted. The butter will begin to foam and become white and frothy, making cracking and popping sounds. This is caused by the evaporation of moisture. Allow it to bubble in this way for about 10 minutes, or until the noises subside.
2. Now, watch this next part of the process carefully. Keep cooking. The butter will foam up a second time. At this point, the milk solids begin to separate and will turn golden brown. When the solids are browned, turn off the heat and let stand for about 15 minutes to allow to cool before pouring into jars. When pouring, strain the ghee through butter muslin. Discard the solids. (Note: Some Ayurvedic cooks use these solids for flavouring other foods.)
3. Store in airtight containers for up to 3 months in the refrigerator or 6 weeks at room temperature.

Prominent Taste: *Sweet*	
If you want to reduce	*eat*
VATA	MORE
PITTA	MORE
KAPHA	LESS

GINGER ELIXIR

◆

Our kitchen staff prefer to give this digestive stimulant
the more romantic name of 'the Aperitif'.
It is consumed in small quantities before lunch or dinner.

15 minutes to prepare

1 large piece fresh root ginger
(about 15cm/6in) *(pungent,*
sweet)

Juice of 3 lemons *(sour, astringent)*
2 tablespoons honey *(sweet)*
Pinch of cayenne *(pungent)*

1. Cut the ginger into 2.5cm/1in pieces and press through a juicer. Blend with the remaining ingredients.
2. Store in an airtight container in the refrigerator for up to 3 days.

Makes about 110ml/4 fl oz

Prominent Tastes: *Sweet, Pungent, Astringent*	
If you want to reduce	*eat*
VATA	SOME
PITTA	LESS
KAPHA	SOME

♥ℒASSI

◆

Lassi is traditionally served at the end of a meal to aid digestion.
It is best consumed in warmer weather.

10 minutes to prepare

SWEET LASSI*

230g/8oz low-fat plain yoghurt
  (sweet, sour)
90g/3oz sweetener** *(sweet)*
470–700ml/1–1½ pints cold
  filtered water

¼ teaspoon cardamom *(pungent,*
  sweet)
2 teaspoons rose water (optional)

1. Combine all the ingredients in a large jar and shake, or place in a liquidizer and blend for 30 seconds.
2. Refrigerate until 30 minutes before serving.

Serves 4 to 6

Prominent Tastes: *Sweet, Sour*	
If you want to reduce	eat
VATA	MORE
PITTA	LESS
KAPHA	LESS

*Omit the sweetener for plain lassi.
For **Vata use rice or barley syrup, for **Pitta** use natural (unrefined) sugar and for **Kapha** use honey.

♥ Morning Chai

♦

For your morning kick-start, try this soothing chai,
individually created for each dosha.

20 minutes to prepare

2 tablespoons loose black tea or 2
black tea bags (optional) *(bitter,*
astringent)

½ teaspoon cardamom *(pungent,*
sweet)

¼ teaspoon cinnamon *(pungent,*
bitter)

¼ teaspoon black peppercorns
(pungent)

¼ teaspoon ground ginger
(pungent, sweet)

60ml/2 fl oz low-fat cow's milk,
soya milk or Rice Dream* *(sweet)*

2 to 4 tablespoons sweetener*
(sweet)

1. In a large saucepan, bring 950ml/1¾ pints of water to a boil. Remove
from the heat.
2. Add the loose tea or tea bags and the spices and steep in the pan or a
teapot for 10 minutes. Add the milk and a sweetener for your dosha.

Makes 950ml/1¾ pints

Prominent Tastes: *Bitter, Pungent*	
If you want to reduce	eat
VATA	LESS
PITTA	SOME
KAPHA	MORE

*For **Vata** use cow's milk and rice or barley syrup, for **Pitta** use cow's milk and natural
(unrefined) sugar, and for **Kapha** use soya milk or Rice Dream and honey.

PANEER CHEESE

◆

Paneer is the Indian form of an old favourite, Italian ricotta. It is easier to digest for all three doshas than most other cheeses. Paneer is firmer than ricotta; it can be fried or used in fillings.

25 minutes to prepare

3.8 litres/7 pints organic milk   950ml/1¾ pints buttermilk

1. In a large saucepan, bring the milk to a boil over medium heat. Do not let it boil over. As it begins to foam, remove the pan from the heat and add the buttermilk. Stir gently. The curds and whey will begin to separate. Set aside and line a colander with a large piece of butter muslin.
2. Pour the cheese into the colander and strain until completely cooled. Gather the ends of the cloth and tightly squeeze it around the cheese, expelling as much liquid as possible. Allow the bag to rest in the colander for an additional hour or two to drain any further liquid.
3. For ricotta, put the cheese in an airtight container and refrigerate immediately. For Paneer, keep squeezing out the liquid until there just isn't any more. Remove the cheese from the cloth and knead for 20 seconds. Press flat in a shallow pan and refrigerate until needed.

Makes 450g/1 lb

Prominent Tastes: *Sweet, Sour*	
If you want to reduce	*eat*
VATA	SOME
PITTA	SOME
KAPHA	LESS

CIRCUS SALSA

◆

*This is a colourful name for a colourful dish. Serve it in summer
when tomatoes, tomatillos and sweetcorn are fresh.*

25 minutes to prepare

450g/1 lb plum tomatoes, chopped
and drained well *(sweet, sour)*

230g/8oz tomatillos, chopped
(optional) *(sweet, sour)*

1 small sweet red onion, finely
chopped *(pungent, sweet)*

3 ears sweet corn, cut from the cob
(sweet)

1 small garlic clove *(all but sour)*

60g/2oz diced green chillies
(pungent)

1 firm avocado, chopped *(sweet)*

Juice of 1 lemon *(sour, astringent)*

Juice of 1 lime *(sour)*

¼ teaspoon sea salt *(salty)*

1 teaspoon natural (unrefined)
sugar *(sweet)*

3 tablespoons chopped fresh
coriander *(pungent)*

1. In a large bowl, toss all the ingredients together. Refrigerate until 1 hour
   before serving.
2. Serve as a side dish with Black Bean Dip (page 41), pitta bread or your
   favourite spicy dish.

Serves 4 to 6

Prominent Tastes: *Sweet, Sour, Pungent*	
If you want to reduce	eat
VATA	MORE
PITTA	LESS
KAPHA	LESS

Date-Raisin Chutney

◆

Try this with Curried Tempeh Salad (page 66).
The sweet chutney offsets the curry to perfection.

20 minutes to prepare

170g/6oz chopped dates *(sweet)*
30g/1oz desiccated coconut *(sweet)*
90g/3oz raisins or currants *(sweet)*
1 teaspoon fennel seeds, bruised in
 a mortar and pestle *(pungent)*
Juice of 1 lemon *(sour, astringent)*

Juice of 1 lime *(sour)*
5cm/2in piece of fresh root ginger,
 grated *(pungent, sweet)*
1 tablespoon finely chopped fresh
 coriander *(pungent)*

1. Toss all the ingredients together in a bowl.
2. Cover and refrigerate for up to 3 days.

Serves 4 to 6

Prominent Tastes: *Sweet, Pungent, Sour*	
If you want to reduce	eat
VATA	SOME
PITTA	SOME
KAPHA	LESS

ℳ𝒶ngo 𝒞hutney

◆

*Chutneys go with almost anything, from Cosmic Curry
Enchiladas (page 109) to Chilli Chickpeas (page 44).
Make this fresh during mango season.*

20 minutes to prepare

2 under-ripe medium mangoes
  (sweet, sour)

1 tablespoon desiccated coconut
  (sweet)

2 tablespoons chopped fresh
  coriander *(pungent)*

1 tablespoon grated fresh root
  ginger *(pungent, sweet)*

⅛ teaspoon sea salt (optional)
  (salty)

⅛ teaspoon hot pepper sauce
  (pungent)

1. Peel the mangoes and carefully cut away from the seed. Cut into small,
   bite-sized pieces. Toss in a bowl with the remaining ingredients.
2. Serve immediately or store, tightly covered, in the refrigerator for up to
   8 hours.

Serves 4 to 6

Prominent Tastes: *Sweet, Sour, Pungent*	
If you want to reduce	*eat*
VATA	MORE
PITTA	LESS
KAPHA	LESS

Tomato Chutney

◆

Try this with any curry dish.

40 minutes to prepare

1 tablespoon vegetable oil, preferably mustard *(pungent)*

2 tablespoon black mustard seeds *(pungent)*

1 garlic clove, minced *(all but sour)*

3 large, firm, ripe tomatoes, coarsely chopped *(sweet, sour)*

230ml/8 fl oz balsamic vinegar *(sour)*

110g/4oz dried minced onion *(pungent, sweet)*

1 teaspoon cinnamon *(pungent, bitter)*

Pinch of sea salt *(salty)*

1 tablespoon black treacle *(sweet)*

2 tablespoons grated fresh root ginger *(pungent, sweet)*

6 whole cloves *(pungent)*

½ teaspoon crushed chillies *(pungent)*

2 tablespoons finely chopped fresh coriander *(pungent)*

1. In a large frying pan, heat the oil for 1 minute. Add the mustard seeds and garlic. When the mustard seeds sputter and pop, add the tomatoes, vinegar, onion, cinnamon and salt. Bring to a boil.

2. Add the treacle, root ginger, cloves and chillies. Bring to a boil again, stirring frequently.

3. Cook for 10 minutes, or until the chutney thickens.

4. Cool to room temperature. Add the coriander. Cover and refrigerate until 1 hour before serving.

Serves 4 to 6

Prominent Tastes: *Pungent, Sweet*	
If you want to reduce	eat
VATA	MORE
PITTA	LESS
KAPHA	SOME

Breakfast

◆

Western nutrition emphasizes the value of breakfast. Taking in fuel to start the day is important, but wait until your appetite calls before filling your stomach. One person may feel ravenous at 6.00 A.M.; another may not feel hunger until 10.00 A.M. Honour your digestive power.

FRUIT AND NUT MUESLI

HOT BARLEY BREAKFAST
CEREAL

HOT BULGUR BREAKFAST
CEREAL

HOT OATS BREAKFAST
CEREAL

HOT RICE BREAKFAST
CEREAL

PLAIN MUESLI

♥Fruit and Nut Muesli
◆

This is a low-fat version of the favourite cereal.

1 hour to prepare

200g/7oz organic rolled oats *(sweet)*

30g/1oz sesame seeds *(sweet)*

30g/1oz nuts, such as chopped almonds *(sweet, bitter)*, chopped walnuts *(sweet)* or pine nuts *(sweet)*

30g/1oz sunflower seeds *(sweet, bitter)*

2 tablespoons cinnamon *(pungent, bitter)*

1 teaspoon cardamom *(pungent, sweet)*

2 tablespoons grated orange peel *(bitter, sour)*

110ml/4 fl oz apple juice concentrate *(sweet, astringent)* or orange juice concentrate *(sweet, sour)*, heated

90g/3oz date pieces *(sweet)*

90g/3oz raisins or currants *(sweet)*

90g/3oz dried mixed fruit pieces *(sweet)*

40g/1½oz desiccated coconut (optional) *(sweet)*

1. Preheat the oven to 160°C/325°F/gas mark 3.
2. In a mixing bowl, combine the oats, sesame seeds, nuts, spices and orange peel. Mix well. Add the juice concentrate and mix well.
3. Spread the mixture on baking trays and bake for about 45 minutes, stirring frequently, until toasted and dry.
4. Allow to cool before adding the fruits and optional coconut. Omit the coconut for even less fat. Store in an airtight container.

Makes about 8 cups

Prominent Taste: *Sweet*	
If you want to reduce	eat
VATA	MORE
PITTA	SOME
KAPHA	LESS

♥Hot Barley Breakfast Cereal
◆

*This is best for **Kaphas** and **Pittas**.*

1 hour to prepare

100g/3½oz organic barley, rinsed
(*sweet*)

Pinch of sea salt (*salty*)

1 teaspoon cinnamon (*pungent,
bitter*)

40g/1½oz currants (optional)
(*sweet*)

Sweetener*, to taste (*sweet*)

Milk*, to taste (*sweet*)

1. In a saucepan, bring 700ml/1¼ pints of water to a boil. Add the barley
   and salt, cover, and simmer over very low heat for 1 hour, or until the
   barley is soft.
2. Add the cinnamon, currants, if using, sweetener and milk and let stand
   covered for 10 minutes. Add more milk, if desired.

Makes 3 cups

Prominent Taste: *Sweet*	
If you want to reduce	eat
VATA	SOME
PITTA	MORE
KAPHA	MORE

*For **Vata** use rice or barley syrup and cow's milk, for **Pitta** use natural (unrefined) sugar
and cow's milk and for **Kapha** use honey and soya milk.

♥Hot Bulgur Breakfast Cereal

◆

This is best for **Vatas** and **Pittas**.

30 minutes to prepare

90g/3oz bulgur wheat *(sweet)*
Pinch of sea salt *(salty)*
1 teaspoon cinnamon *(pungent, bitter)*

40g/1½oz currants (optional) *(sweet)*
Sweetener*, to taste *(sweet)*
Milk*, to taste *(sweet)*

1. In a saucepan, bring 340ml/12 fl oz of water to a boil. Add the bulgur and salt, cover and simmer over very low heat for 25 minutes.
2. Add the cinnamon, currants, if using, sweetener and milk and let stand covered for 10 minutes. Add more milk, if desired.

Makes 2 cups

Prominent Taste: *Sweet*	
If you want to reduce	eat
VATA	MORE
PITTA	MORE
KAPHA	LESS

*For **Vata** use rice or barley syrup and cow's milk, for **Pitta** use natural (unrefined) sugar and cow's milk and for **Kapha** use honey and soya milk.

❤Hot Oats Breakfast Cereal
◆

*This porridge is good for **Vatas** and **Pittas**.*

30 minutes to prepare

60g/2oz organic rolled cut oats *(sweet)*

Pinch of sea salt *(salty)*

1 teaspoon cinnamon *(pungent, bitter)*

40g/1½oz currants (optional) *(sweet)*

Sweetener*, to taste *(sweet)*

Milk*, to taste *(sweet)*

1. In a saucepan, bring 700ml/1¼ pints of water to a boil. Add the oats and salt, cover and simmer over very low heat for 25 minutes.
2. Add the cinnamon, optional currants, sweetener and milk and let stand covered for 10 minutes. Add more milk, if desired.

Makes 3 cups

Prominent Taste: *Sweet*	
If you want to reduce	eat
VATA	MORE
PITTA	MORE
KAPHA	LESS

*For **Vata** use rice or barley syrup and cow's milk, for **Pitta** use natural (unrefined) sugar and cow's milk and for **Kapha** use honey and soya milk or Rice Dream.

♥Hot Rice Breakfast Cereal

◆

This is good for all doshas.

30 minutes to prepare

100g/3½oz organic basmati rice
 (sweet)

Pinch of sea salt *(salty)*

1 teaspoon cinnamon *(pungent, bitter)*

40g/1½oz currants (optional)
 (sweet)

Sweetener*, to taste *(sweet)*

Milk*, to taste *(sweet)*

1. In a saucepan, bring 230ml/8 fl oz of water to a boil. Add the rice and salt, cover and simmer over very low heat for 20 minutes.
2. Add the cinnamon, currants, if using, sweetener and milk and let stand covered for 10 minutes. Add more milk, if desired.

Makes 1½ cups

Prominent Taste: *Sweet*	
If you want to reduce	*eat*
VATA	SOME
PITTA	SOME
KAPHA	SOME

*For **Vata** use rice or barley syrup and cow's milk, for **Pitta** use natural (unrefined) sugar and cow's milk and for **Kapha** use honey and soya milk or Rice Dream.

♥Plain Muesli
◆

*If served with skimmed milk or low-fat plain yoghurt, this is a
great almost fat-free breakfast.*

45 minutes to prepare

200g/7oz organic rolled oats *(sweet)*

1. Preheat the oven to 160°C/325°F/gas mark 3.
2. Spread the oats on a baking tray and bake for about 45 minutes, stirring
   frequently, until toasted and dry. Allow to cool. The muesli may be
   stored in an airtight container for several weeks.

Makes 2 cups

Prominent Tastes: *Sweet, Sour, Pungent*	
If you want to reduce	eat
VATA	MORE
PITTA	SOME
KAPHA	LESS

Chapter

5

PURIFICATION AND REJUVENATION

EATING TO DETOXIFY/EATING TO REJUVENATE

The idea that we store impurities in our mind-body system as a result of a stressed metabolism is new to science. Western medicine has only recently begun addressing issues like free radicals as an important feature of ageing and illness. We are now learning that while our cells are functioning, we create very reactive chemicals that alter proteins and carbohydrates in our tissues, rendering them indigestible. Over time, this stuff clogs up our cells, leading to disease and death.

Ayurveda seems to have anticipated this discovery thousands of years ago when it described a toxic substance called *ama* as the product of incomplete digestion. Over time, *ama* accumulates, blocking the channels of circulation. When the channels are obstructed, the life force *(prana)* cannot reach the cells and tissues, leading to degeneration.

There are many classic signs and symptoms of accumulated *ama*. These include:

fatigue

weak digestion

bad breath

a coated tongue

general pain

weakness

difficulty concentrating

depression

irritability

If we are experiencing any of these symptoms, it's a sign that we've been accumulating toxicity, which is making our minds dull and our bodies weak. If we see a medical doctor at this time, complaining of fatigue or discomfort, any laboratory test that is ordered is likely to be normal. According to Ayurveda, this is the best time to put some attention on cleansing the system, because it is much harder to re-establish health once a definite imbalance has got a foothold. Clearing the mind and body from *ama* at this stage is true disease prevention and health promotion.

WHEN TO CONSIDER A DETOXIFICATION PROGRAMME

Any time we are challenged physically or emotionally, we have the tendency to accumulate toxicity. If we have recently been through a major upheaval, such as a change in residence, job or relationship, the chances are that we have used up some life energy and could use a simplified nutritional plan for a while. Any intense event such as a graduation or wedding is usually accompanied by some temporary disruption in our eating habits and sleeping pattern. These are times that our digestive power is weakened and *ama* can accumulate. Long-distance travelling is another experience that can be energy consuming, and it is helpful to follow a detoxification programme for a day or two after a long trip.

If we have faced a recent health problem such as surgery or infection, we almost certainly have accumulated emotional and physical stress and can use some detoxification. This is particularly true if we have needed to be on one or more medicines for a time.

If we have been over-eating recently and are carrying a few more pounds than we'd prefer, it probably reflects some lack of mind-body integration due to subtle toxin accumulation. Shifting to a detox programme for a few days will re-establish our mind-body connection. Whenever we find that our energy level is not what we think it should be and our biorhythms are out of sync, it's a good idea to slow things down for a couple of days and focus on purifying with an *ama*-reducing programme.

THE AMA-REDUCING PLAN

The basic plan is to simplify. By taking in only foods that are easy to metabolize, we allow our digestive forces to focus on burning up accumulated toxins. In Ayurveda, the principle of digestive power is known as *agni*. This Sanskrit word also means 'fire', which is an interesting way to think about our ability to digest what we take in. If our internal 'fires' are strong, we can burn what we take in, creating abundant energy and healthy tissues. If our 'fires' are weak, our digestion becomes delicate and we aren't able to create the energy we need. We also generate *ama*, which can be thought of as the smoke and charred remains of a weak fire. The goal of the detoxification programme is to 'reset' our digestive fires and burn up accumulated impurities.

The food we eat and the manner and environment in which we eat it all influence our digestive power. During the *ama*-reducing programme, we pay attention to all these aspects of eating and digesting. These are the recommendations:

- All food should be freshly prepared, nutritious and appetizing; avoid tinned foods and leftovers.

- Foods should be lighter in quality, such as rice, soups and lentils.

- Favour freshly steamed or *very* lightly sautéed vegetables.

- Avoid fried foods.

- Avoid cold foods and drinks.

- Minimize dairy products.

- Avoid fermented foods and drinks. These include vinegar, pickled condiments, cheeses and alcohol.

- Keep oils to a minimum.

- Favour lighter grains, such as barley or millet.

- Avoid refined sugars; small amounts of honey may be used but should not be cooked with or heated.

- Avoid most nuts, which are oily, heavy and usually salted; sunflower, pumpkin or sesame seeds may be taken in small amounts.

- If you cannot avoid animal products, favour the white meat of turkey or chicken; avoid red meats, particularly pork and beef.

- Drink plenty of fluids during the detox programme. We recommend preparing a ginger tea by grating 1 teaspoon of fresh root ginger into 470ml/16 fl oz of boiling water. If you prepare this in a Thermos flask in the morning, you can sip it throughout the day. Ginger, known in Ayurveda as the 'universal medicine', is cleansing and purifying. If you can't find fresh ginger, sip warm water throughout the day.

- Aloe vera juice is another readily available natural detoxifier. Taken in a dose of two tablespoons twice per day for five to seven days, it is restorative to the immune system, particularly after a course of antibiotics.

AMA-REDUCING HERBS AND SPICES

Certain herbs and spices are very effective in helping the body detoxify. Herbs with a predominantly bitter taste help to reduce *ama* while those with a pungent taste help to 'burn it up'. Readily available bitter herbs include turmeric, coriander, rosemary, dill and fenugreek. Herbs and spices with a pungent taste can be classified as being warm or hot. The warm spices, such as cumin, cardamom, coriander, basil and fennel, will not irritate people with a tendency towards high **Pitta**. The hot spices like cayenne, black pepper, dried ginger and mustard can quickly incinerate *ama* but should be used cautiously if **Pitta** is predominant.

LENGTH OF THE CLEANSING PROGRAMME

The *ama*-reducing plan is recommended three times per year, at the beginning of autumn, winter and spring. People with predominantly **Vata** constitutions should follow the diet for one week at a time. People with **Pitta** constitutions may follow it for two to four weeks. If you are predominately **Kapha,** you can benefit from the *ama*-reducing programme intermittently throughout the year, as it most closely resembles a standard **Kapha**-balancing regimen.

Although many of the general principles of the *ama*-reducing diet are beneficial at all times, it wouldn't be any fun to be always so restrictive. When you feel your energy level is rising and your digestion improving, begin to add some dairy products, oils, nuts and heavier grains. Occasional helpings of fried or fermented foods can add variety to a meal.

LIQUID DIET

An easy way to follow a cleansing diet is to take everything in the form of a liquid or purée for a day. This means drinking the fresh juices of fruits and vegetables throughout the day and taking thin soups that have been blended. Whenever possible, use freshly squeezed rather than bottled or frozen juices, as *prana* is always highest in fresh foods.

Apples and citrus fruits are available year round in most areas and easily make fresh juices. Pitted fruits (peaches, plums, nectarines) also make wonderful juices, but will not be available in all seasons. With a good juicer or extractor, delicious juices can be made from carrots, beetroot and celery. Mixing fruit and vegetable juices together can create very appetizing combinations, such as apple-carrot or apple-beetroot.

Making up a thin vegetable soup and then blending it can provide a nourishing meal that is also very easy to digest. Adding some mung beans to the blend ensures that all the tastes and nutritional components are included.

We recommend using a liquid diet for one day at a time. If your mind-body type is predominantly **Vata,** and you feel fine going for a day without solid foods, then following the programme one day per month is recommended. If you are a **Pitta,** two or three times per month is of value. If you are a **Kapha** type, then as often as one day per week can be helpful in reducing the tendency to accumulate toxins.

$\mathcal{V}$EGETABLE $\mathcal{B}$ROTH

◆

40 minutes to prepare

1 carrot, cut into pieces *(sweet, pungent)*

2 celery stalks, cut into pieces *(bitter, astringent)*

140g/5oz chopped spinach *(bitter)*

1 potato, quartered *(astringent)*

Dash of asafoetida (hing) *(pungent)*

Pinch of tarragon *(pungent)*

470ml/16 fl oz purified water

1 tablespoon soy sauce *(astringent, salty)*

1. In a soup pan, combine all the ingredients and bring to a boil. Simmer for 20 minutes.
2. Strain the vegetables for a clear broth or blend in a food processor or with a hand-held soup blender for a thick soup.

Makes 700ml/1¼ pints

Prominent Tastes: *Pungent, Bitter, Astringent*	
If you want to reduce	*eat*
VATA	SOME
PITTA	SOME
KAPHA	MORE

Beet Broth

◆

1 hour to prepare

950ml/1¾ pints purified water
1 tablespoon vegetable bouillon
   powder *(all)*
900g/2 lbs beetroot, washed and
   chopped *(bitter, sweet)*

2 pinches grated fresh root ginger
   (pungent, sweet)
2 pinches grated orange zest *(bitter)*
Pinch of asafoetida (hing) *(pungent)*

1. In a soup pan, combine all the ingredients and bring to a boil. Simmer
   for 30 to 40 minutes, until the beetroot is soft.
2. Strain for a clear beetroot broth or blend in a food processor or with a
   hand-held soup blender for a thick soup.

Makes 950ml/1¾ pints

Prominent Tastes: *Sweet, Bitter, Pungent*	
If you want to reduce	*eat*
VATA	SOME
PITTA	SOME
KAPHA	MORE

GREEN SOUP

◆

20 minutes to prepare

1.4kg/3 lbs spinach, washed and chopped *(bitter)*

2 celery stalks, cut into pieces *(bitter, astringent)*

2 tablespoons chopped parsley *(pungent, astringent)*

2 tablespoons chopped fresh coriander *(pungent, astringent)*

950ml/1¾ pints purified water

1 tablespoon soy sauce *(astringent, salty)*

2 pinches tarragon *(pungent)*

1. In a soup pan, combine all the ingredients and bring to a boil.
2. Strain for a clear broth or blend in a food processor or with a hand-held soup blender for a thick soup.

Makes 950ml/1¾ pints

Prominent Tastes: *Bitter, Pungent, Astringent*	
If you want to reduce	*eat*
VATA	SOME
PITTA	MORE
KAPHA	MORE

Vegetable Juice

◆

15 minutes to prepare

1 carrot *(sweet, pungent)*
1 beetroot *(bitter, sweet)*
280g/10oz spinach *(bitter)*

Pinch of sea salt
Purified water, as necessary for
 thinning

1. Press the vegetables through a juicer. Discard the pulp. Add salt. Thin with water, if desired.
2. Drink immediately.

Makes 230–470ml/8–16 fl oz

Prominent Tastes: *Bitter, Sweet*	
If you want to reduce	*eat*
VATA	SOME
PITTA	SOME
KAPHA	SOME

REJUVENATION

According to Ayurveda there are certain foods that are rich in *prana* and therefore recommended on a daily basis. These *prana*-rich foods are **milk, almonds, honey** and **ghee** (clarified butter). Adding just a small amount of these nourishing substances to your diet will improve your vitality. A great energy booster that can be taken in the morning or later in the day is an Almond-Banana milkshake. If you are recovering from a debilitating illness, trying to gain weight or just wanting an energy boost, this drink is delicious and satisfying.

Almond-Banana Milkshake

◆

230ml/8 fl oz semi-skimmed or
whole milk *(sweet)*

1 whole banana *(sweet)*

2 tablespoons almond butter *(sweet, bitter)*

1 teaspoon honey *(sweet)*

½ teaspoon ghee *(sweet)*

Blend all of the ingredients together.

Serves 1

Prominent Taste: *Sweet*	
If you want to reduce	*eat*
VATA	MORE
PITTA	SOME
KAPHA	LESS

There is an entire Ayurvedic science of revitalizers, or *Rasayanas,* which has explored the rejuvenative value of foods for thousands of years. Some of the fruit and herb formulas described thousands of years ago are available today. The most famous one is known as *Chavan Prash,* which has a fruit known as *amalaki (Emblic myrobalan)* as its major constituent. This fruit has *ten times* the vitamin C per gram of pulp than an orange and, when combined with more than 40 other herbs and spices, is a powerful restorative. It has potent antioxidant properties, which may explain its long-held reputation as an anti-ageing formula. It is usually available as a herbal jam that can be taken plain, spread on bread or mixed with warm milk or water.

If you put your attention on reducing the toxins in your life and accepting only nourishing influences, you will notice a big improvement in your physical and mental clarity. Taking the time to focus on detoxification and rejuvenation pays off. You'll accomplish things more easily because you will have more energy and will enjoy whatever you're doing more.

High Energy Snack

◆

10 minutes to prepare

60g/2oz crushed toasted almonds *(sweet, bitter)*

40g/1½oz toasted desiccated coconut *(sweet)*

2 tablespoons toasted sesame seeds, plus additional for rolling *(sweet)*

3 tablespoons honey* *(sweet)*

90g/3oz dried fruit (currants, dates) *(sweet, sour, astringent)*

1. In a food processor, combine the almonds, coconut, 2 tablespoons sesame seeds, honey and dried fruit and process for about 30 seconds, until well blended and pulverized.
2. By the teaspoonful, form into balls and roll in additional sesame seeds. These can be stored in the refrigerator in an airtight container for several days.

Makes 10 to 12 medium-sized balls

Prominent Tastes: *Sweet, Astringent*	
If you want to reduce	*eat*
VATA	MORE
PITTA	SOME
KAPHA	SOME

*For **Pitta** and **Kapha** use honey and for **Vata** use maple syrup.

Tofu-Nut Burger

◆

30 minutes to prepare

450g/1 lb firm tofu, drained well *(sweet, astringent)*

30g/1oz toasted pine nuts *(sweet)*

30g/1oz toasted almonds *(sweet, bitter)*

30g/1oz toasted sunflower seeds *(sweet, bitter)*

1 egg *(sweet)*

2 tablespoons soy sauce *(astringent, salty)*

30g/1oz dry wholemeal bread crumbs, plus additional bread crumbs *(sweet)*

30g/1oz chopped celery *(bitter, astringent)*

1 tablespoon ghee (optional) *(sweet)*

1. Preheat the oven to 200°C/400° F/gas mark 6.
2. In a large bowl, crumble the tofu.
3. Place the pine nuts, almonds and sunflower seeds in a food processor and process until pulverized. Combine with the tofu, egg, soy sauce, 30g/1oz bread crumbs and celery. Form into patties.
4. Place additional bread crumbs in a small bowl. Place each patty in the bowl with the bread crumbs, patting gently on each side, to pick up the crumbs. Fry in ghee, if desired, or bake in the oven for 10 minutes.

Serves 2 to 4

Prominent Tastes: *Sweet, Bitter, Astringent*	
If you want to reduce	eat
VATA	MORE
PITTA	SOME
KAPHA	LESS

Sweet Lassi

◆

5 minutes to prepare

230g/8oz low-fat plain yoghurt
(sweet, sour)

110ml/4 fl oz rose water or purified
water

¼ teaspoon cardamom *(pungent,
sweet)*

¼ teaspoon cinnamon *(pungent,
bitter)*

1 tablespoon honey or maple syrup
(sweet)

Combine all the ingredients and shake or stir well. Make fresh daily.

Serves 2 to 4

Prominent Tastes: *Sweet, Pungent*	
If you want to reduce	*eat*
VATA	SOME
PITTA	LESS
KAPHA	LESS

Spinach and Paneer Casserole

◆

45 minutes to prepare

1 teaspoon ghee *(sweet)*

2 large leeks, washed and chopped *(pungent, sweet)*

1.4kg/3 lbs fresh washed spinach *(bitter)*

1 teaspoon each cumin, coriander, turmeric *(pungent)*

1 tablespoon soy sauce *(astringent, salty)*

170g/6oz Paneer cheese, cut into small pieces (page 168) *(sweet, sour)*

1 egg *(sweet)*

60g/2oz crushed toasted almonds *(sweet, bitter)*

30g/1oz bread crumbs *(sweet)*

1. Preheat the oven to 180°C/350°F/gas mark 4.
2. In a large frying pan, heat the ghee to the smoking point. Sauté the leeks until soft and browned. Add the spinach and cook until slightly wilted. Remove from the heat.
3. Add the remaining ingredients except 2 tablespoons of bread crumbs.
4. Pour into a lightly oiled casserole dish and sprinkle with the remaining bread crumbs. Bake for 25 minutes, or until the crumbs are browned and the casserole is bubbling.

Serves 2 to 4

Prominent Tastes: *Sweet, Bitter, Pungent*	
If you want to reduce	eat
VATA	SOME
PITTA	SOME
KAPHA	SOME

Chapter

6

COOKING SINGLE

Living alone has its nourishment hazards: why is it that the most important body we know, our own, gets the least attention? We eat on the run, eat junk food, eat less than we should, eat *leftovers* or eat out. Cooking single can be a rewarding, self-nourishing ritual. Sit down to a well-balanced meal by yourself at a beautifully laid table. Look at the food and give thanks for the gifts of life and sustenance. While you are eating, concentrate on the act of eating itself. Chew slowly, swallowing each bite before you lift another forkful into your mouth. Feel the food enter your cells as life force. Don't watch television. Don't read. Don't answer the phone. Become the ritual of eating. It's difficult, isn't it? We are used to distraction, diversion and entertainment. We hurry through the meal, thinking there must be something more important to do than sit alone in a room with a plate of spaghetti. We bolt down the meal, throw the plate in the dishwasher and run out the door.

In this chapter, we offer a few menus and recipes for one. Take care of yourself.

MENU

PASTA PRIMAVERA *(sweet, astringent)*
SALAD OF BABY GREENS WITH YOUR DOSHIC DRESSING
(bitter, astringent, sour)
WHOLEMEAL CHAPATTIS *(sweet)*

Pasta Primavera

◆

25 minutes to prepare

1 carrot *(sweet, pungent)*

1 broccoli floret *(bitter, astringent)*

1 celery stalk *(bitter, astringent)*

5 green beans *(sweet, astringent)*

1 tablespoon oil, olive for **Vata** or
   Pitta, sunflower for **Kapha** *(sweet)*

30g/1oz fresh basil *(pungent)*

¼ teaspoon asafoetida (hing)
   (pungent)

Juice of 1 lemon *(sour, astringent)*

4 sun-dried tomatoes, chopped
   (sweet, sour)

110g/4oz pasta of your choice,
   cooked and drained *(sweet)*

Grated Parmesan cheese *(sweet)*

1. Cut the carrot, broccoli, celery and green beans into bite-sized pieces. In a hot frying pan, sauté quickly in the oil. Toss in the basil, asafoetida, lemon juice and tomatoes.
2. Serve over warm pasta, adding Parmesan cheese.

Serves 1

Prominent Tastes: *Sweet, Astringent*	
If you want to reduce	eat
VATA	MORE
PITTA	SOME
KAPHA	LESS

M E N U

A DIFFERENT PESTO *(all)*
PASTA *(sweet)*
STEAMED VEGETABLE *(bitter, astringent)*
SPICED BAKED APPLE *(sweet)*

A Different Pesto

◆

20 minutes to prepare

30g/1oz fresh spinach, washed and stemmed *(bitter)*

½ avocado, cut into pieces *(sweet)*

30g/1oz fresh coriander *(pungent)*

30g/1oz fresh basil *(pungent)*

30g/1oz fresh parsley *(pungent, astringent)*

2 tablespoons lemon juice *(sour, astringent)*

2 tablespoons pine nuts *(sweet)*

Salt *(salty)*

Pepper *(pungent)*

110g/4oz pasta of your choice, cooked and drained *(sweet)*

Combine all the ingredients except the pasta in a food processor and blend well. Serve with warm pasta.

Serves 1

Prominent Taste: *All*	
If you want to reduce	eat
VATA	MORE
PITTA	SOME
KAPHA	SOME

Spiced Baked Apple

◆

45 minutes to prepare

1 Cox's or Granny Smith apple
  (sweet, astringent)
½ teaspoon ghee *(sweet)*
1 teaspoon ground pine nuts *(sweet)*
1 teaspoon maple syrup *(sweet)*

2 pinches ground cardamom
  (pungent)
⅛ teaspoon cinnamon *(pungent)*
60ml/2 fl oz unfiltered apple juice
  (sweet)

1. Preheat the oven to 200°C/400°F/gas mark 6.
2. Peel the top of the apple about ⅓ of the way down and cut out a 2.5cm/1in piece from the centre core. Mix the ghee, nuts, maple syrup, cinnamon and cardamom together and put in the well in the centre of the apple.
3. Place in a small baking dish with the apple juice, cover with foil and bake about 30 minutes. Uncover, baste with apple juice and bake until soft, about 15 more minutes.

Serves 1

Prominent Taste: *Sweet*	
If you want to reduce	*eat*
VATA	SOME
PITTA	SOME
KAPHA	SOME

Chapter

7

MENU PLANNING

The following suggested menus are derived from the recipes in this book. We offer these to help you create balance throughout your week in planning Ayurvedic meals.

BREAKFAST

We acknowledge that breakfast is different for everyone. However, we suggest that the following items often be included for balance:

> *Muesli or hot cereal with a pinch of salt*
> *(sweet, salty)*
>
> *Morning Chai (bitter, astringent, pungent)*
>
> *Yoghurt (sweet, sour)*
>
> *Fruit (sweet, astringent)*

LUNCH OR DINNER

According to Ayurveda, lunch should be the main meal of the day. We understand that busy lifestyles often prevent our eating at home or even eating where or when we wish. The options below give you examples of the variety and balance to look for in your meals out or in home meal planning. Time usually allows for more attention to dinner preparation. A calm, gentle atmosphere adds to the experience. Remember, *avoid stress!* Mealtime is a celebration, not a drama. Choose items carefully, relax and enjoy.

A Different Pesto (with pasta)
Spinach with Gorgonzola
French Bread
Lemon Bars

◆

Veggie Burgers
Salad Greens with Doshic Dressing of Choice
Baked Apples

◆

Mushroom Stroganoff (with basmati rice)
Classic Chopped Salad
Anadama Bread
Glazed Pear Tart

◆

Cheeseless Lasagne
Leeks and Limas
Italianate Muffins
Chocolate Chip Cookies

◆

Cosmic Curry (with basmati rice)
Cucumber Raita
Wholemeal Chapattis
Cranberry Bliss Balls

◆

Acorn Squash Soup
Chapatti Crisp Salad
Ginger-Treacle Cookies

◆

Vegetable Chow Mein
Orange Almond Rice
Fresh Blueberry Cake

◆

Tofu Satay (with basmati rice)
Orange Almond Spinach
Naan
Shakti Date Balls

◆

Red Lentil Dhal
Curried Tempeh Salad
Pitta Bread
Pear-Date Raita
Baklava

◆

Watermelon Soup
(with Beetroot and Orange)
Vegetarian Niçoise
Goody Muffins
Date Bars

Chapter

8

ORCHESTRATING
A FEAST

We describe tantra as a 'composition in consciousness with four-part harmony: *Kriya*, ritual; *Carya*, demeanour; *Yoga*, integration of mind, body and spirit; and *Anuttara*, understanding'. These practices, when carried with you into the kitchen, create an atmosphere of wholeness and unity. When we begin to understand the completeness of our being through these practices, we begin to share in the unity and spirit of all things.

Although we express the idea that all meals are an opportunity for celebrating nourishment and that every act of eating can be a special occasion, we acknowledge that there are moments when more time is available and more thought given to the experience.

Orchestrating a meal gives you the opportunity to compose a tantric melody. It can be sung by a choir. It can be whispered, like the chanting of monks. It is a gift of creation and a process of celebration.

One of the most important aspects of the creation of a meal is organization. If you are baking bread, making a sumptuous dessert, cooking rice and creating canapés, you are probably looking forward to an evening soirée, Sunday brunch or a gathering of friends. This not only means cooking a meal but arranging flowers, ironing napkins and blow-drying your hair. Don't despair. It can come together easily if certain organizational steps are taken, if your heart is in the right place and if you relax.

Preparing Ayurvedically balanced menus includes the six tastes, *churans,* accompanying music, flowers and a beautiful table. The spirit with which you begin is the spirit that carries through the entire experience. Are you nervous? Not to worry. Begin with the ritual (thought) that this is a divine moment in creation. Make your shopping list while sipping tea and listening to melodic music. Plan a menu with six tastes represented, list the ingredients then look out the window at a flower. Remind yourself that this is a party, not a summit meeting, and you are honoured to be the party giver.

While you are shopping, buy fresh flowers (or collect them from nature if you can) – some for the table and some for you in the kitchen. Take your own recycled bags with you. If you are able to shop at farmers' markets, smile and talk with the farmers; let them know how much you appreciate the beautiful produce grown with their love.

Upon arriving home, take all your ingredients out of the bags and pile them up on the counters, arranging a tableau of peppers, potatoes, tomatoes, nectarines and flowers, or whatever you have chosen. To look at the bounty of produce on your counters is to partake in the abundance that is life. Place a fresh flower in a vase, light a candle and prepare yourself to become the task of washing vegetables, kneading dough and beating eggs. Listen to music. Be in love. With whom? With yourself and life, of course.

So, here you are, set to go. The menu is planned. The shopping is done. The candle is lit. The ritual is begun. Now what? If you are not already comfortable in the kitchen, this moment can be disconcerting. How is this done so that everything comes out at the same time? How can I do all this and still have time to rest, bathe and arrange the table?

Look at your menu. It looks something like this:

Acorn Squash Soup

Mushroom Stroganoff over basmati rice

Classic Chopped Salad

French Bread

Glazed Pear Tart

Begin to take it apart by its components. The bread takes the longest, but it does not need to go into the oven for at least 1½ hours, after it has risen. The squash needs to be baked. The pears need poaching. The salad needs washing and chopping. Make the dressing. Defrost the pastry.

Make an outline of what has to be done. For example:

Preheat the oven.

Cut the squash and bake it.

Make the bread dough and set it aside to rise (near a warm oven).

Peel the pears and poach in the juices.

Brush the mushrooms, wash the herbs for the Stroganoff.

Wash the vegetables for the chopped salad.

When the bread dough is doubled, knock it back, make loaves and set aside to rise.

Remove the pears from the pan to cool and reduce the juice to syrup.

Remove the cooked squash from the oven and cool.

Chop the Stroganoff ingredients and set aside.

Chop the salad ingredients and place in a bowl.

Place the risen loaves in the oven.

Make the dressing.

Finish the soup.

Turn off the heat under the reduced syrup and cool.

Take a break, have lunch, sip tea.

Arrange the flowers.

Remove the bread from the oven to cool.

Defrost the pastry dough.

Finish the tart.

Take another break. The main body of work is finished. Have a bath, meditate, relax. Make sure you give yourself time for this. Your nurturing of yourself is every bit as important as the nourishment you are preparing for your friends or family.

Refreshed, you re-enter your studio of nourishment and begin the final preparation. Lay the table, light the candles, plump up the sofa cushions.

When your guests arrive, you are happy and relaxed and your kitchen is sparkling clean, awaiting last-minute dinner preparations; all you have left to do is

Finish the Stroganoff.

Cook the rice.

Toss the salad.

Be charming.

Invite friends into the kitchen to talk while you finish your preparations. Let them share in your enjoyment of the abundance in which they are about to take part: the crusty loaves cooling on racks on the counter; the prepared salad in a beautiful bowl, the dressing in a little jar beside it; the vegetables, ready to be sautéed, nested on a colourful platter. Your temple of creation includes the energy of your guests at this point, and they can't help but be honoured by your effort.

We request one final thing: enjoy yourself.

CELEBRATE

◆

Food is a celebration of life. Whether you are packing your lunch in the morning, planning a dinner party for eight or creating a wedding feast for 100, give attention to the details in every step. Honour the ritual of preparation; honour the ceremony of eating; honour yourself and the process of transformation that you are while you eat. You are a beautiful creation, composed of body, mind and spirit. When you are in your studio of nourishment, you have the opportunity to contribute richness and harmony to the act of eating. As a cook, you hold in your hands the tools of sustenance. As an artist of nourishment, you are creating sacred space and sacred food. Be on holy ground. Be at peace. Be love itself. Be well.

APPENDIX

Glossary of Terms

AGNI : digestive power

AMA : toxic residues of incompletely metabolized substances

AYURVEDA : science or knowledge of life

BRAHMAN : spirit; pure potentiality

CHURANS : spices blended for each individual dosha

DHARMA : purpose in life

DOSHA : mind-body principle

VATA : the dosha responsible for all movement in the body

PITTA : the dosha responsible for metabolism or transformation in the body

KAPHA : the dosha responsible for structure and lubrication of the body

PRANA : life force

RAJAS : principles of energy and activity

RASA : the essence of body tissue; taste; emotions

SATTVA : principle of creativity and clarity

TAMASIC : principle of inertia, resistance

TANTRA : the web of life; practices to become aware of the spiritual nature of all things

ANUTTARA : understanding

CARYA : demeanour

KRIYA : ritual

YOGA : integration of mind, body and spirit

VEDA : knowledge of creation in its unmanifest and manifest expressions

Suggested Reading

The books listed below are valuable resources for anyone interested in the further study of Ayurveda. We heartfully thank our teachers for providing this information. We recommend these books for your home library:

Ageless Body Timeless Mind
Deepak Chopra, M.D.

Ayurveda: The Science of Self-Healing
Vasant Lad

The Ayurvedic Cookbook
Amadea Morningstar with Urmila Desai (Lotus Press)

The Book of Ayurveda: A Holistic Approach to Health and Longevity
Judith H. Morrison

The Healing Cuisine: India's Art of Ayurvedic Cooking
Harish Johari

Perfect Weight: The Complete Mind-Body Program for Achieving and Maintaining Your Ideal Weight
Deepak Chopra, M.D.

Tantra for the West
Marc Allen

The Yoga of Herbs: An Ayurvedic Guide to Herbal Medicine
David Frawley and Vasant Lad

Balance of Tastes Chart

Of the six tastes, sweet, sour and salty are the most predominant in our usual diet. Pungent, bitter and astringent are taken in less quantity but are very important for their balancing influence on our physiology. Pungent taste is commonly obtained through the hot spices such as pepper, chillies, ginger and mustard but is also present in many herbs, such as basil, sage and cinnamon. The bitter taste is very common in nature and most medicinal herbs are predominantly bitter, but we are naturally less attracted to bitter taste and tend to use it in smaller quantities as a culinary spice. Although most of us don't love a bitter taste, it has a very important influence on digestion by serving to cleanse our system of toxins. Leafy greens are the most important food source of bitter taste, but it is also prominent in commonly used herbs and spices such as dill, fenugreek, turmeric and coriander. Astringent taste is relatively rare. Lentils, beans and dhals are the most available sources of astringent taste. The puckery feeling in your mouth after a great cup of black tea demonstrates the astringent influence. Fruits such as pomegranate, apples and cranberries are astringent. Herbs and spices that carry the astringent taste include sage, cinnamon and nutmeg.

The following Balance of Tastes Chart characterizes commonly available foods, herbs and spices according to their Ayurvedic energetics. For a more detailed description of their specific effects, we refer you to the recommended reading list on page 208.

VEGETABLES	TASTE	VATA	PITTA	KAPHA
Artichokes	sweet, astringent	Less	More	Some
Asparagus	sweet, bitter, astringent	Some	More	More
Aubergines	bitter	Some	Some	Some
Bean Sprouts	astringent, sweet	Less	More	More
Beans (Green)	sweet, astringent	Less	More	More
Beetroot	bitter, sweet	More	Some	More
Broccoli	bitter, astringent	Less	More	More
Brussels Sprouts	astringent, sweet	Less	More	More
Cabbage	astringent, sweet	Less	More	More
Carrots	sweet, pungent	More	Some	More
Cauliflower	sweet, astringent	Some	More	Some
Celery	bitter, astringent	Some	More	More
Chillies (hot pepper)	pungent	More	Less	More
Coriander	pungent	More	More	More
Courgettes	sweet	More	More	More
Cucumbers	sweet, astringent	Some	More	Less
Fennel	pungent	More	Less	More
Jerusalem Artichokes	sweet	More	More	Less
Jicama	sweet	More	More	Less
Lettuce	bitter, astringent	Less	More	More
Mushrooms	sweet, astringent	Less	More	More
Mustard Greens	pungent, bitter	More	Less	More
Okra	sweet	More	More	Some
Onions, cooked (Leeks, Spring onions, Chives, Shallots)	sweet, pungent	Some	Some	More
Onions, raw (Leeks, Spring onions, Chives, Shallots)	sweet, pungent	Less	Less	Less
Parsley	pungent, astringent	More	Some	Some
Peas (Green or) Mange-tout	sweet, astringent	Less	More	More
Potatoes	astringent	Less	Some	Some
Radishes	bitter	More	Some	More
Seaweed	salty, astringent	More	Some	Some
Spinach	bitter	Some	Some	Some

VEGETABLES	TASTE	VATA	PITTA	KAPHA
Squash				
Acorn	sweet	Less	Some	Some
Winter	sweet	Less	Some	Less
Sweetcorn	sweet	Less	Some	Some
Sweet Peppers	sweet, astringent	Less	Some	Some
Sweet Potatoes	sweet	More	Some	Less
Tomatoes	sweet, sour	Less	Some	Some
Turnips/Swedes	astringent	Less	Some	More

GRAINS	TASTE	VATA	PITTA	KAPHA
Barley	sweet	Some	More	More
Buckwheat	sweet	Some	Some	Some
Corn	sweet	Some	Some	Some
Couscous	sweet, astringent	Less	More	Less
Millet	sweet	Some	Some	Some
Muesli				
Dried grains	sweet, astringent	Less	Some	More
Oats	sweet	More	More	Less
Quinoa	sweet, astringent	Some	Some	More
Rice				
Basmati	sweet	More	More	Some
Brown	sweet	More	Some	Less
Refined, White	sweet	Some	Some	Less
Rye	sweet, astringent	Less	Some	Some
Spelt	sweet, astringent	More	More	Some
White Flour	sweet, astringent	Less	Less	Less
Wholemeal Flour	sweet, astringent	More	More	Less

HERBS/SPICES	TASTE	VATA	PITTA	KAPHA
Allspice	pungent	More	Less	More
Anise	pungent	Less	Less	More
Asafoetida (hing)	pungent	More	Less	More
Basil	pungent	More	Some	More
Bay Leaves	pungent	More	Less	More
Black Pepper	pungent	Some	Less	More
Calamus	pungent	More	Less	More
Caraway	pungent	More	Some	More
Cardamom	pungent, sweet	More	Some	More
Catnip	pungent	Some	Some	Some
Cayenne	pungent	Some	Less	More
Chamomile	pungent, bitter	More	More	More
Cinnamon	pungent, bitter	More	Some	More
Cloves	pungent	More	Some	More
Coriander	pungent, bitter	More	More	More
Cumin	pungent	More	Some	More
Dill	pungent	Some	Some	Some
Fennel	pungent	More	More	Some
Fenugreek	bitter	More	Less	More
Garlic	all but sour	More	Less	More
Ginger	pungent, sweet	More	Less	More
Horseradish	pungent	Some	Less	More
Hyssop	pungent, astringent	More	Less	More
Italian Seasoning	pungent	More	Less	More
Lemon Verbena	pungent, sour	Some	Some	Some
Lemon grass	pungent, sour	Some	Some	Some
Marjoram	pungent	More	Less	More
Mint	pungent	Some	Some	Some
Mustard	pungent	Some	Less	More
Nutmeg	pungent, astringent	More	Some	Some
Oregano	pungent	More	Less	More
Paprika	pungent	Some	Some	Some
Peppermint	pungent	Some	Some	Some
Poppy Seeds	pungent, astringent, sweet	More	Less	More

HERBS/SPICES	TASTE	VATA	PITTA	KAPHA
Rosemary	pungent, bitter	More	Some	More
Saffron	pungent	Some	Some	Some
Sage	pungent, astringent	More	Less	More
Spearmint	pungent	Some	Some	Some
Star Anise	pungent, sweet	More	Less	More
Tarragon	pungent	More	Less	More
Thyme	pungent	More	Less	More
Turmeric	bitter, pungent, astringent	Some	Some	More

NUTS/SEEDS	TASTE	VATA	PITTA	KAPHA
Almonds	sweet, bitter	More	Less	Less
Brazil Nuts	sweet	More	Less	Less
Cashews	sweet	More	Less	Less
Coconut	sweet	Some	More	Some
Hazelnuts	sweet	More	Less	Less
Lotus Seeds	sweet, astringent	Less	More	Less
Macadamia Nuts	sweet	More	Less	Less
Mustard Seeds	pungent	More	Less	More
Peanuts	sweet, astringent	Less	Less	Some
Pecans	sweet, bitter	More	Less	Less
Pine Nuts (Piñon)	sweet	More	Some	Less
Pistachios	sweet	More	Less	Less
Pumpkin Seeds	sweet	Some	Some	Some
Sesame Seeds	sweet	More	Some	Some
Sunflower Seeds	sweet, bitter	Some	More	Some
Walnuts	sweet	More	Less	Less

FRUITS	TASTE	VATA	PITTA	KAPHA
Apples	sweet, astringent	Some	More	More
Apricots	sweet, sour	Some	Less	Some
Avocados	sweet	More	Some	Less
Bananas	sweet, astringent	Some	Less	Less
Blueberries	sweet, astringent	More	More	Less
Cranberries	astringent, sweet	Less	More	More
Cherries	sweet, sour	More	Less	Less
Dates	sweet	More	More	Less
Figs	sweet, astringent	More	More	Less
Grapefruit	sour	More	Some	More
Grapes	sweet, sour	More	More	Less
Lemons	sour, astringent	More	Less	Less
Lemon, Orange Zest	bitter	Less	More	More
Limes	sour	More	Less	Less
Mangoes	sweet, sour	More	Some	Less
Melons	sweet	Less	More	Less
Nectarines	sweet, sour	More	Some	Less
Oranges	sweet, sour	Some	Some	Less
Papayas	sweet	More	Some	Some
Peaches	sweet, sour	Some	Less	Less
Pears	sweet	Some	More	Some
Pineapples	sweet, sour	More	More	Less
Plums	sweet, sour	Some	Some	Less
Prunes	sweet, sour	More	More	Some
Pomegranates	sweet, astringent, sour	Some	More	Some
Raisins, Currants, Sultanas	sweet	Less	Some	More
Raspberries, Blackberries	sweet, sour	More	Some	Less
Strawberries	sweet, sour, astringent	More	More	Less
Tangerines	sour, sweet	Some	Less	Some

PULSES	TASTE	VATA	PITTA	KAPHA
Aduki Beans	sweet, astringent	Some	More	More
Black Gram (Indian)	sweet, astringent	Less	More	Some
Broad Beans	sweet, astringent	Less	More	More
Chickpeas	sweet, astringent	Some	Some	Less
Kidney Beans	sweet, astringent	Some	Some	Some
Lentils	sweet, astringent	Less	Some	More
Lima Beans	sweet, astringent	Some	More	More
Mung Beans	sweet, astringent	More	More	Some
Pinto Beans	sweet, astringent	Less	Some	Some
Soyabeans	sweet, astringent	Less	Some	More
Tofu	sweet, astringent	Some	More	Some
Split Peas	sweet, astringent	Less	Some	Some

DAIRY	TASTE	VATA	PITTA	KAPHA
Butter	sweet	More	More	Less
Buttermilk	sour, astringent	More	Less	Some
Cheese	sweet	Some	Some	Less
Cottage Cheese	sweet	More	More	Less
Cream	sweet	More	More	Less
Ghee	sweet	More	More	Some
Ice Cream	sweet	Less	Less	Less
Kefir	sour	More	Some	Some
Milk	sweet	More	More	Less
Paneer Cheese	sweet, sour	Some	Some	Some
Sour Cream	sweet, sour	More	Less	Less
Yoghurt	sweet, sour	More	Less	Less

MEAL/FISH/ POULTRY	TASTE	VATA	PITTA	KAPHA
Beef	sweet	Some	Less	Less
Chicken, Turkey	sweet	Some	Some	Some
Duck	sweet	More	Less	Less
Lamb	sweet	Some	Less	Less
Pork	sweet	Less	Less	Less
Venison	sweet	More	Less	Less
Fish	sweet, salty	More	Some	Less
Shellfish	sweet	More	Less	Less
Animal Products				
Eggs	sweet	More	Less	Less

OILS/FATS	TASTE	VATA	PITTA	KAPHA
Almond	sweet, bitter	More	Less	Less
Avocado	sweet, astringent	More	Some	Less
Corn	sweet	Less	Some	Some
Coconut	sweet	Some	More	Less
Flaxseed/Linseed	pungent, sweet	More	Less	More
Lard	sweet	Some	Some	Less
Margarine	sweet	Less	Some	Some
Mustard	pungent	Some	Less	More
Olive	sweet	More	Some	Less
Peanut	sweet	Some	Less	Some
Rapeseed	sweet	Less	Some	More
Safflower	sweet, pungent	More	Some	More
Sesame	sweet	More	Less	Less
Soy	sweet, astringent	Some	Some	Some
Sunflower	sweet	Some	Some	More

SWEETENERS	TASTE	VATA	PITTA	KAPHA
Crystallized Sugar	sweet	Some	Some	Some
Honey	sweet	Some	More	More
Lactose – Milk, Sugar	sweet	Some	Some	Some
Malt, Rice, Barley Syrup	sweet	More	More	Some
Maple Syrup	sweet	More	More	More
Natural (Unrefined) Sugar	sweet	More	More	Some
Treacle	sweet	More	Less	Less
White Sugar	sweet	Less	Less	Less

FLAVOURINGS/ CONDIMENTS	TASTE	VATA	PITTA	KAPHA
Carob	sweet, astringent	Some	More	More
Chocolate	pungent, bitter	Some	Less	Less
Cornflour	sweet	Some	Some	Some
Mayonnaise	sour, sweet	Some	Less	Less
Mustard	pungent	More	Less	More
Salt	salty	Some	Less	Less
Soy Sauce	astringent, salty	Some	Less	Less
Vegetable Seasoning Powder	all	Some	Some	Some
Vinegar	sour	Some	Less	Less

BEVERAGES	TASTE	VATA	PITTA	KAPHA
Alcohol	pungent, sweet, bitter, sour	Some	Less	Less
Coffee	pungent, bitter	Less	Less	Some
Fizzy Drinks	sweet	Less	Less	Less
Fruit Juices				
Citrus	sweet, sour	More	Less	Less
Other	sweet, astringent	Less	More	More
Herbal Teas				
Cinnamon,				
Ginger etc.	spicy	More	Less	More
Green, Mint etc.	astringent	Less	More	More
Milk and Dairy (see Dairy)				
Mineral Water				
(Carbonated)	bitter	Less	More	More
Tea (Black, Regular)	bitter, sweet, astringent	Less	More	More
Vegetable Juices				
Carrot	sweet, astringent	More	Less	More
Cucumber	sweet, astringent	More	More	Less
Spinach	bitter, astringent	Less	Less	More

INDEX

Index

THE CHOPRA CENTER
FOR WELL BEING

Ginna Bragg and David Simon strive to fulfil their *dharma* at The Chopra Center for Well Being in La Jolla, California. The Center offers unique holistic health care and educational programmes, which have been developed under the guidance of Drs. Deepak Chopra and David Simon. All the programmes of the Center are guided by the principle that health is more than the absence of disease, but rather a state of dynamic harmony among body, mind and spirit.

Ginna provides delicious, nutritious meals for guests and course participants at the Center and teaches inspiring weekly cookery classes. For more information on classes and programmes at the Center, write to:

The Chopra Center for Well Being
7630 Fay Avenue
La Jolla, California 92037 U.S.A.

For information on healing-related seminars, books, videotapes, audiotapes, CD ROMs and products in Europe, please contact:

Contours
44 Fordbridge Road
Ashford
Middx TW15 2SJ
UK
Tel: +44-181-564 7033
Fax: +44-181-897 3807